LIVING THE DREAM!

"Another Year in Paradise!"

by

Father Charlie Urnick

This is a collection of sermons given at St. John the Baptist Catholic Church in Laughlin, Nevada, from July 2010 until July 2011. To hear the current sermons, please join us for Mass. We love company! Our Weekend Mass schedule is as follows:

Saturday 4:00 PM
Mass at Don's Celebrity Theatre in the Riverside Resort,Laughlin, Nevada

Saturday 6:00 PM
Mass at St. John the Baptist Catholic Church, 3055 El Mirage Way, Laughlin, Nevada

Sunday 8:00 AM
Mass at St. John the Baptist Catholic Church 3055 El Mirage Way, Laughlin, Nevada

Sunday 10:00 AM
Mass at Don's Celebrity Theatre in the Riverside Resort,Laughlin, Nevada

Sunday 12:00 Noon
Mass at Don's Celebrity Theatre in the Riverside Resort,Laughlin, Nevada

St. John the Baptist Catholic Church
P.O. Box 31230 Laughlin Nevada 89028

TO ALL WHO READ THIS BOOK -

I am the happiest Catholic priest in the whole world! I was ordained as a Catholic priest in New Jersey on May 25, 1974 and I have reached 44 years as a priest this year (2018). In fact, I am already looking forward to celebrating my 50th Anniversary of Priestly Ordination on May 25, 2024. I think one of my favorite pictures from that time in my life is this picture of my Mom (Mary) and me standing at the doors of Our Lady of Mercy Catholic Church in Park Ridge, New Jersey, my home parish, where I offered my First Mass on the day following my ordination. Golly, I looked so young back then! I was 26 years old when this picture was taken. The years go by so quickly.

My current assignment is **Paradise**, otherwise known as **Laughlin, Nevada**! I have been assigned here as Administrator of St. John the Baptist Catholic Church since July 1, 2008. As far back as I can remember, my dream has been to serve as a priest in the **Diocese of Las Vegas**, and here I am living my dream along the banks of the beautiful Colorado River! Yes, this is really **Paradise** for me! And I am so very grateful to be serving here.I have been publishing collections of my sermons to share my happiness as I continue to discover the joys of living here in Laughlin and serving at St. John the Baptist Catholic Church. With this new book, my third, I will complete my **TRILOGY**! I will have published a sermon for every Sunday in the three-year cycle of the Catholic Lectionary. **Of course, I intend to continue preaching sermons and writing books for as long as I live!** But these three books mark a very special three years of my life here in the Diocese of Las Vegas.And I want to express deep a debt of gratitude to the new bishop of the Diocese of Las Vegas – Most Reverend George Leo Thomas – for his gracious encouragement to me to publish this particular book at this particular time. I think he knows how much I appreciate his personal interest and his personal kindness. I want to thank him very much for allowing me to express myself through the publication of these sermons. And I hope Bishop Thomas will enjoy reading them as much as I have enjoyed writing them and sharing them.

DREAMS REALLY DO COME TRUE!
("My First Year in Paradise!")
My sermons from July 2008 until July 2009

DREAMS REALLY
DO COME TRUE!
"My First Year in Paradise"
(Laughlin, Nevada)

Father Charlie Urnick

LIVE! LOVE! LAUGH! LAUGHLIN!
("The Dream Continues in Paradise!")
My sermons from July 2009 until July 2010

LIVE! LOVE!
LAUGH! LAUGHLIN!
"The Dream Continues
in Paradise!"

Father Charlie Urnick

LIVING THE DREAM!
(Another Year in Paradise!)
My sermons from July 2010 until July 2011
The current book you are reading!

Welcome to my world!

I have always been blessed with happiness because of the truly amazing people in my life, and since this book is the third one in my Trilogy **(and definitely not the last!)**, I really want and need to single out some of those amazing people for praise and thanks:

- My Mom and Dad who brought me into this world a long, long time ago. My Dad lived to see me almost complete my teenage years. He died in 1967 when I was 19 years old. My Mom lived to see me ordained as a priest and shared so much of my love for Las Vegas, Laughlin and all of Nevada throughout the years. My Mom died in 2006, but she is very much a part of my life even now. There is a very special bond between a mother and her son. **Ask any son, or any mother, and they know what I am talking about.**

- The parishioners of St. John the Baptist Catholic Parish in Laughlin, Nevada, who continue to give me so much **hope** and **joy** and **love**, and who have to listen to me preach almost every weekend of the year! **They are awesome!**

And they have made me feel so much at home here since the very first day I arrived. By the way, I first called Laughlin **"Paradise"** in my sermon on 23 November 2008! And it will be **"Paradise"** forever in my mind until I get to the **OTHER** Paradise (Heaven)! And I really do intend to get there!

- The snowbirds and visitors who come to Laughlin from all over the world and who worship with us either at our church on the hill or in the Riverside Casino, and who bring me bulletins and news from churches around the world. St. John the Baptist Catholic Church here in Laughlin is a very special and unique ministry. We are the **ONLY CATHOLIC CHURCH IN THE UNITED STATES** (and maybe even **IN THE WHOLE WORLD!**) which meets every weekend in a **CASINO!** Why, we even have our own casino chips! And we even have valet parking at the casino! How cool is that?

Our unique and beautiful souvenir casino chips!

- My brother **Michael** who really has been one of the best and most influential behind-the-scenes forces in my life, always encouraging me to be my best self, patiently **(sometimes)** calling me to account when I am not, and always inspiring me to see and hear elements of life I might never have noticed without him. It is undeniably true that it is to Michael that I owe the push to actually sit down and write my first book. And I equally owe Michael the credit for encouraging/prodding/pushing /shoving me to write my second and third books! Michael is really and truly an awesome and talented brother! **Michael, I'm so blessed and so glad we're family!** You sometimes have the wisdom of Solomon to share with me in my life! And **sometimes**, I really do listen to you! No, really, I sometimes do!

- My "illegitimate son" **Eddie** who shows up on several pages of this book because his genuine goodness and youthful enthusiasm make me the proudest Pa in the world. **Eddie is clearly my much-loved "illegitimate son!"** Because of him, I have learned so much about the incredible joys and worries of being a **father** with a small **"f"** which in turn, I think, has made me a much better **Father** with a capital **"F"** for my parishioners! There's an old saying that if you love someone, you sometimes want to kill him. I love you, son! (NLPLC). **Eddie, I'm so blessed and so glad we're family!**

- My "other son" **Andy** who discovered his Las Vegas family on his way to LA some years ago. Eddie and Andy had been roommates and friends and brothers for almost forever, so it was very natural that Andy should move into our family. Sometimes he looks like the kid next door, and other times he looks like a psychotic serial killer! **Andy, I'm so blessed and so glad we're family!**

- The four of us - **Myself, Michael, Eddie and Andy** - have chosen to be more than friends. **We've chosen to be family!** If you can appreciate what that means to me, no further explanation is necessary. If you can't appreciate what that means to me, no further explanation is possible.

A photo of our Family!
Charlie, Andy, Eddie and Michael

REMEMBER AS FAR AS EVERYONE KNOWS, WE ARE A NICE NORMAL FAMILY

14

- My friends, **Paul** and **Charlie,** who keep me honest and truthful and smiling and hugged. I don't think they realize how much their friendship has contributed to my life, but I owe them big time, **really big time!** They are really the very first friends I made in Las Vegas when I moved out West in 2008. And they remain some of the closest people in my life!

- My friend, **Bruce Ewing**, whose own writings online are so good and so inspirational for me to read, and who shares a beautiful outlook on life and grace with me. From **"Forever Plaid"** to the days of the **"Phat Pack"** and beyond, Bruce continues to be an influence for grace and good in my life! And he knows the best places to eat!

- My friend **Mike**, from the **Mike Hammer Comedy Magic Show** up in Las Vegas is an truly outstanding example of God putting the **best people** into my life. Talented, funny, sincere, giving, and so many other adjectives describe him so well. I can't begin to add up how many Tuesday or Wednesday nights I have spent laughing and smiling and eating and just hanging out with him on Fremont Street over the past several years! I never knew it could be so much fun to "GET HAMMER'D!"

- My friend (and brother!) **John**, who moved from scenic **Sheridan, Wyoming**, to Nevada to pursue his career in magic. We share a passion for magic, and we have spent countless Tuesday and Wednesday nights meeting in Las Vegas and checking out the magic shows, or just enjoying a leisurely people-watching walk along the Strip. Along with Michael, and Eddie, and Andy, John keeps me feeling so young and so hopeful.

- And here in Laughlin, my friend, **Steve**, who gets dragged into so many of my local parish adventures, yet never complains and always helps to make the adventures a lot of fun. I think I've eaten more meals with Steve than with anyone else out here! And he did an awesome job of putting my boxed office furniture together! That man has the patience of a saint! And the organizational abilities of a world-class CEO!

- And also in Laughlin, my friend **Pat** who moved here from New Jersey to enjoy the sun and warmer climate. Pat had worked as my secretary in New Jersey for 14 years….and she still doesn't mind helping out in the parish here and sharing an occasional meal with me.

- And across the country in the land of Connecticut, I have to thank my friend and brother **Kyle** for keeping a prayerful watch over me and sharing so much of his life and wisdom with me. **His patriotism, enthusiasm, and tireless courage are so inspirational to me!**

CEO'S SNOWFLAKE TEST

S				2
IT	17.55 ▼ 0.03	S&P 2341.88 ▼ 2.14	
00@ 23.02 UNCH	GENERAL ELECTRIC (GE) 1.		

- The priests of my past who taught me so much by their preaching, and so much more by their lives: Father Charlie O'Connor, Msgr. Tom Kleissler, Father Ed Duffy, Father Gerry McGarry, Msgr. Dave Casazza, Father Francis Byrne, Father Ken St. Amand, Msgr. James Turro, Father Chuck McCusker, Father Charlie Hudson, Msgr. Peter O'Connor, Msgr. Caesar Orrico, Msgr. Mike Fitzpatrick, Msgr. Charles Lillis, Father Robert Hunt, Father Ed Ciuba, Msgr. Harold Darcy, Father Steve Feehan, Msgr. Carl Hinrichsen, and Father Edward Hinds.

- And all those people who have ever said to me on their way out of Mass here in Laughlin: **"Have you ever thought of putting your sermons together in a book?"** Well, for the third time now, I have!

I began serious work on this collection of sermons from my third year in Laughlin back in March 2013, and I completed the basic structure by the summer of 2013, spending almost five months revising and revisiting a year of sermons at St. John the Baptist Catholic Church in Laughlin. It has definitely been a labor of love doing this! For those who hear me regularly, you will recognize the development of some common themes and messages. You will see some wonderfully awesome recurring characters in my sermons because they are in my life. For various reasons in the Diocese of Las Vegas, it has taken 5 years for this book to see publication. I am honored that our newly-appointed bishop – The Most Reverend George Leo Thomas – has given his nod of approval for this book to finally be published.

I never have to make up my stories, they happen to me!

Welcome to my world!

Most of my sermon material is purely original, but sometimes it has been inspired by things I have seen or read in books, magazines, newspapers or on the internet. I apologize if I have inadvertently used someone else's material without giving proper credit. I do occasionally read sermon ideas by Father Anthony Kadavil online and the works of Father Anthony de Mello always provide inspiration in this book. Thanks to my parishioners who travel frequently, I have been able to read parish bulletins from more than 900 parishes across the USA and around the world. So many of my sermon ideas come from reading these slices of parish life.

A portion of the profits from the sale of this book **($1.00 from every book sold)** will be donated to **St. John the Baptist Catholic Church** to assist in the current works and activities of the **best little parish in the world!** We are proud to be a little outpost of the Diocese of Las Vegas serving all those who live in or visit

Laughlin, and the surrounding communities in Nevada, Arizona, and California.

Over the years, I've collected a number of sayings which I have found to be helpful, humorous, thoughtful and guiding. I gladly share them with you at the start of this journey through my third year in Laughlin and the entire year that follows. Perhaps reading some of these sayings might prepare you for the mind and spirit behind the sermons that follow. I hope you enjoy the journey with me, it's going to be an awesome ride! If you liked my first book **DREAMS REALLY DO COME TRUE!,** and if you made it through my second book **LIVE! LOVE! LAUGH! LAUGHLIN!** , then I think you will also enjoy this new book **LIVING THE DREAM!** Some of these sayings appeared in my first and second books, but I love them so much that I want to repeat them and add to them here!

"I wouldn't like to have lived without ever having disturbed anyone!"
(Catherine Doherty)

"Relationships are built on trust; trust begins by sharing."
(Christian Mueller)

"Laughter is the sound of assumptions breaking."
(Michael Goudeau)

"For personal growth, you should do something every day that scares you!"
(Kevin Lynch...as he coaxed me onto his Harley!)

"Consider any man that you can help your friend, and double friend that man so selfless as to offer help to you."
(Rod McKuen)

"I think when you are somewhere, you oughta be there, 'cause it's not about how long you stay in a place, it's about what you do while you're there. And when you go, will the place where you've been be any better off for your having been there?"
(Chris Stevens/John Corbett in the show "Northern Exposure")

"Someday, we'll look back on this, laugh nervously, and change the subject!"
(Ken Mason)

"Live!...Love!...Laugh!"
(David Kesterson)

"There is nothing wrong with pointing out the flaws of people you care about as long as you are in their lives long enough to assist them in overcoming their flaws."
(Michael Rene Serrano, 25 July 2009)

"Of course you did!"....."Really?"
(Michael Rene Serrano)

"You're stuck with me - wherever I go, whatever I do - you're coming along for the ride!"
(Eddie Gelhaus, 29 March 2010))

"Haha! I'll deny the stories and burn the pics!"
(Andy Greene, 30 September 2010)

"If you're ever in a jam, I'll be there to lend a helping hand."
(Jason Haskins, 6 August 2012)

"Pray for me! What harm could it do?"
(Father Charlie)

"You're such a character!"
(Jason Haskins, 24 May 2013)

"See you in church!"
(Father Charlie)
"Be good, be strong, be you!"
(Father Charlie)

"It's so nice...It must be Paradise!"
(Father Charlie)

"Dreams really do come true!"
(Father Charlie)

"Live!...Love!...Laugh!...Laughlin!"
(Father Charlie)

"Living the Dream"
(Murray SawChuck)

"Thanks for joining me in this crazy adventure called Life!"
(Charles Hoffmaster, 28 February 2013)

**This is a review of my first book.
You may find some insight into my style and my dreams here!**

DREAMS REALLY DO COME TRUE! My First Year in Paradise (Laughlin, Nevada)

by Father Charlie Urnick (Published February 19, 2011)
Reviewed by Jim M. Guynup, Christ the King Parish, Las Vegas, Nevada

In the southern tip of Nevada, there lies a town about 90 minutes from the center of Las Vegas where a man named Don Laughlin bought this piece of land by the Colorado River in 1964 and founded the Riverside Casino at which he then offered a complete chicken dinner for 98 cents! And despite his not wanting it, the townfolk insisted on calling it Laughlin. Over 50 years later a vivacious priest with an effervescent smile starts his love affair with Laughlin. He was ordained 1974 in New Jersey where he demonstrated his love for preaching and teaching for over 34 years. Then a lifelong dream became reality when his prayers were answered and he was transferred to Laughlin in the Diocese of Las Vegas.

Father Charlie Urnick loves to preach and write and one can easily feel that with every word he says or writes. His first venture in book-writing includes his sermons from 2008-2009 which have been described by Amazon.com as **"folksy wisdom"** and to that I would like to add if you enjoyed Fulton J. Sheen, then reading this book is an absolute must!

What Father Charlie manages to do is make relevant the readings in the liturgical year plus inject humor and add some love for his beloved Laughlin, including the food and then maybe even give us a household tip! For instance, one that I have since shared with many friends: **"If you cannot find your car in the parking lot, just put the keychain up to your chin and press the sounding button and with your body as the external antenna, it will find your car immediately"**

Father Charlie Urnick addresses all types of issues including trust, love, death, plants, Las Vegas, Lent, and, yes, even casinos, and the origin of Angel Food cake. He has many photos of his various adventures though I wish some of them could have been in color. Maybe next time hopefully. Since he also had a distinguished career in the Air Force, hopefully the next one that he is now planning will include more of that.

What struck me most about the book is his appreciation for many things that we take for granted, whether it is his love for a favorite food or the beauty of his town. His words about Laughlin and about our Catholic Christian Faith come so alive in this book that I hope each of you will experience it yourselves for a truly memorable summer reading experience.

14th Sunday in Ordinary Time - "C"

4 July 2010

FIRST READING: Isaiah 66:10-14
PSALM: Psalm 66:1-7, 16, 20
SECOND READING: Galatians 6:14-18
GOSPEL: Luke 10:1-12, 17-20

This sermon was preached at St. Francis of Assisi Parish in Henderson, Nevada, on this date during my brief tenure there as Temporary Administrator.

In the Gospel today, Jesus appoints 72 disciples to go out and prepare the way for Him.

We received word on Friday that Bishop Pepe has assigned Father Steve Hoffer as a parochial vicar here at St. Francis. In this day and age, having **TWO** parochial vicars is almost unheard of! Having two parochial vicars as young as Father John and Father Steve is infinitely more rare! But our status as a growing parish surely justifies it. So we are very grateful that as of August 1st, St. Francis of Assisi will have two young parochial vicars.....**and one aging administrator!**

On this July 4th weekend, I know I don't need to give a long sermon and you don't need to sit for one either. But I'd like to point out a bit of inspiration as we celebrate our 234th birthday as a free and independent nation. The Declaration of Independence, which was signed 234 years ago, begins with these stirring words:

"We hold these truths to be self-evident, that all men are created equal, that they are endowed by their Creator with certain unalienable Rights, that among these are Life, Liberty and the pursuit of Happiness."

234 years later, we all need to remember that from the very beginning, our nation has acknowledged that there is a **CREATOR**, and that He is the Source of all our rights.

And that we are all endowed by our Creator with the right to **LIFE**, **LIBERTY** and the **PURSUIT OF HAPPINESS**. The Declaration of Independence states that all of this is **SELF-EVIDENT**, meaning that any thinking person should be able to see it.

So, as we celebrate this July 4th weekend, it's good for us to give thanks to our **CREATOR**, and to thank Him for giving us **LIFE**, and **LIBERTY**, and allowing us to **PURSUE** our happiness. It should be **SELF-EVIDENT** to all of us that God has given us so very much in the course of our lives. It's good to think about this.

There are websites for everything these days. There's one for waiters called **WAITER'S REVENGE** where waiters and waitresses can post the most annoying things that customers in restaurants have done to them.....and what funny or disgusting things they have done to get even! It's worth checking out, but it may make you a little worried about eating out for awhile!

There are many sites for preachers, and one listed some comments about sermons. I really enjoyed that one, even though it made me think a bit about my own preaching style. Here are some of the comments I found:

The definition of a good sermon: It should have a good beginning. It should have a good ending. And they should be as close together as possible.

A sermon should be modeled on a woman's dress: long enough to cover the subject, but short enough to be interesting.

A rule of thumb for preachers: If after ten minutes you haven't struck oil, stop boring!

A woman said, "Father, that was a very good sermon!" The priest says, "Oh, I have to give the credit to the Holy Spirit." And the woman replied, "It wasn't THAT good!"

A priest, whose sermons were very long and boring, announced in the church one Sunday that he had been transferred to another church, and that it was Jesus' wish that he leave that week. The congregation got up and sang, "What a Friend We Have in Jesus!"

So, with that in mind, on to today's sermon.....

There once was a king who offered a prize to the artist who would paint the best picture of **PEACE**. Many artists tried. The king looked at all the pictures. But there were only two he really liked, and he had to choose between them. One picture was of a calm lake. The lake was a perfect mirror for peaceful towering mountains all around it. Overhead was a blue sky with fluffy white clouds. All who saw this picture thought that it was a perfect picture of peace. The other picture too had mountains, but they were rugged and bare. Above was an angry sky, from which rain fell and in which lightning played. Down the side of the mountain tumbled a foaming waterfall. This did not look peaceful at all! But when the king looked closely, he saw behind the waterfall a tiny bush growing in a crack in the rock. In the bush a mother bird had built her nest. There, in the midst of the rush of angry water, sat the mother bird on her nest...in perfect peace.

Which picture do you think won the king's prize? The king chose the second picture. Do you know why? **"Because,"** explained the king, **"peace does not mean to be in a place where there is no noise, trouble or hard work. Peace means to be in the midst of all those things and still be calm in your heart. This is the real meaning of peace."**

Today's Gospel reading from St. Luke tells us that the 72 disciples were sent out two-by-two to bring His message of peace. They were to strengthen and support each other, to depend on God for what they needed, and to share God's message with those to whom they were sent. They were even reminded that they would not always be successful, but that they should never give up, or become cynical. They had a message that was incredibly valuable. And they were never to stop offering it to the world.

The lessons for us are simple and obvious. Think of that picture of peace, realize that your Faith gives you the ability to face whatever life throws at you, learn to depend on God more than anyone else and never give up on sharing your Faith with those around you in whatever ways you can.

Like Jesus' original disciples, we too have a message for the world that is incredibly valuable. And we are never to stop offering it to the world. It is a message that is more powerful, more life-changing, more hopeful than even our Declaration of Independence! It can bring us to eternal life, complete liberty from sin, and everlasting happiness!

God bless you!

Father Charlie & Father John sharing a few smiles!

15th Sunday in Ordinary Time - "C"

11 July 2010

FIRST READING: Deuteronomy 30:10-14
PSALM: Psalm 69:14, 17, 30-31, 33-34, 36-37
SECOND READING: Colossians 1:15-20
GOSPEL: Luke 10:25-37

The Parable of the Good Samaritan reminds us that sometimes God can send us His help through the most unlikely characters in our lives.

So glad to be here in Paradise this weekend! Father John is over in Germany and I've got a couple of other priests covering the Henderson parish this weekend. Hopefully everything will go smoothly up there! **It is real nice to have a weekend without driving!** One of the things I've noticed because of my constant travels lately is that people are sending or leaving me more notes than usual. Some of them are really weird and some of them are really funny! I'm thinking of making them into a sermon someday. **I think you'd be amazed and amused what people write to priests these days**. I did have a funny experience in Henderson last weekend. I was talking with some people outside of church after one of the Masses and this lady comes up to me and hands me a pen. Since I

34

hadn't asked for a pen and I wasn't planning on writing anything, it seemed a little odd. But I took it from her and looked at it, and noticed there was writing on it. **It was an advertisement for a beauty salon!** So I asked her if she worked there. She told me she did, and then added..."**Come see me, I can fix that hair!**"

Other than worrying about my hair, sometimes people have an interest in the training of a priest. Every now and then I get questions from people like **"Did you have to take a class in sermon-writing?"** or **"What was it like in the seminary?"** Today's Gospel brings to mind some of my most vivid seminary memories and they actually are connected to our class in sermon-writing.

The year was 1970. I was in my 2nd year in the seminary, and someone came up with the brilliant idea that we should act out the Gospel passages in our sermon-writing class, videotape them, and discuss them. One week, we were given the **Parable of the Good Samaritan** as our text. My class divided up the parts. Some were the robbers, one was the Jewish priest, one was the Levite, one was the Good Samaritan. I was given the part of the man going from Jerusalem to Jericho. Video cameras in those days were bulky and unreliable, and that day was a particularly bad one for the camera man. As I walked, my classmates tackled me and very realistically beat me up in the classroom, but then the cameraman asked for a retake because he had problems with the video camera. So we did it again, and again, and finally after I had been beaten up 4 times we went through the whole parable. At the end of the class, we sat around talking about the video and the parable. Each person related how he felt during the re-enactment. Finally, they asked me what my favorite part of the parable was, and I told them **"When they stopped hitting me and someone came to help me."**

The Good Samaritan is one of the most famous of Jesus' parables, even though it is told only in Luke's Gospel. There is something appealing about it even today, 2000 years after Jesus told it. I think much of its appeal and lastingness comes from the fact that we **WANT** to believe that kindness can come from anyone, no matter how unlikely. I have a feeling that the parable of the man going from Jerusalem to Jericho who was beaten by robbers could be written in a new way for each generation of people and still have the same meaning - an unexpected act of kindness means a lot.

Perhaps the story could be told of the old man going from Las Vegas to Laughlin who gets a flat tire on 95 in a howling dust storm in temperatures around 115 degrees. And the BMW's and the MERCEDES' speed past him until a pierced/tattooed teen with a multi-colored Mohawk haircut stops his motorcycle and changes the tire for the old guy.

And the amazing thing about an unexpected act of kindness is that it has a way of changing a person's outlook on people who look or act or believe differently. It really helps to break down the stereotypes that we sometimes hold in our minds. People of all races, groups, beliefs, ages, colors, and lifestyles can be downright neighborly. And in fact, that's what Jesus is telling us in the Gospel today. **We need to be neighbors to those who need neighbors.**

We all know how good it feels when someone does something kind for us. This week, try to do one act of kindness for someone else. **Do something, anything, to make a difference for good!**

God bless you!

My Chalice and Paten ready for celebrating the Holy Eucharist.

16th Sunday in Ordinary Time - "C"

18 July 2010

FIRST READING: Genesis 18:1-10
PSALM: Psalm 15:2-5
SECOND READING: Colossians 1:24-28
GOSPEL: Luke 10:38-42

Martha and Mary point us in the direction of realizing God's goodness all the time in a variety of circumstances.

An amazing and very hot week in Paradise. I think we're going to hit around 120 degrees this weekend. I guess it is an incentive to be good and faithful. After all, if it's this hot in Paradise....just imagine what that other place in eternity could be like!

On Tuesday evening, I found myself in a large classroom with 60 children between the ages of 4 and 9. It was the **Vacation Bible School** up at St. Francis in Henderson/Las Vegas. Before I spoke to the kids, the VBS leader was getting them ready for the evening. She had them all stand facing me, and told them she wanted them to repeat whatever she yelled by yelling it back at her as loud as they could. **I knew then that I was in for an awakening!** So she yelled: "**GOD IS GOOD!**" And all the 60 kids yelled back with a deafening: **"GOD IS GOOD!"** She told them to do it louder, and they did. And then she said she knew they could do it even louder, and they did! The room was rocking (and my head was throbbing!) as the 60 kids yelled out as loud as they possibly could: **"GOD IS GOOD!"** Then she moved on to Part Two.....having them yell out after her, **"ALL THE TIME!"** until they were yelling it as loudly as they possible could. Then, she had them combine the two! She would say **"WHAT?"** and they would yell **"GOD IS GOOD!"** and then she'd say **"WHEN?"**, and they'd yell back **"ALL THE TIME!"** And after she got them all worked up, she pointed to me and said, **"And now, Father Charlie, wants to say a few words to you."** I'm not sure what I said, I couldn't hear myself, my eardrums were gone! But I do remember asking the kids if they had any questions for me, and the first one I got was from a 6 year boy who asked me, **"FatherCharlie, is it fun to be a priest?"** I told him, just what I would tell any of you, **"It sure is!"** I wonder if we could all try it now. Pretend you're between the ages of 4 and 9.....and let's do some yelling! What? **"GOD IS GOOD!"** When? **"ALL THE TIME!"**

A man attending a crowded church service refused to take off his hat when asked to do so by the ushers. Others also asked him to remove his hat, but he remained obstinate. The preacher was perturbed, too, and waited for the man after the service. He told the man that the church was quite happy to have him as a guest, and invited him to join the church, but he explained the traditional rules regarding men's hats and said, "I hope you will conform to that practice in the future." "Thank you," said the man. "And thank you for taking time to talk to me. It is good of you to invite me to join the congregation. In fact, I joined it three years ago and have been coming regularly ever since, but today is the first time that anyone paid any attention to me. After being an unknown for three years, today, by simply keeping my hat on, I have had the pleasure of talking with the ushers, several of the parishioners, and you. Thanks!" Our scripture for this Sunday is about welcoming – about hospitality. It is about noticing the other and being attentive to the other. In our first reading, Abraham and Sarah go out of their way to entertain the stranger, and they receive God's blessing. In the gospel, Martha and Mary receive Jesus in their home at Bethany, each in her own characteristic way.

A story is told about an advertising executive at Reader's Digest. In spite of her successful career, she had felt emptiness in her life. One morning, during a breakfast meeting with her marketing consultant, she mentioned that emptiness. **"Do you want to fill it?"** her colleague asked. **"Of course I do,"** she said. He looked at her and replied, **"Then start each day with 15 minutes of** prayer." She looked at him and said, **"Don, you've got to be kidding. If I tried that, I'd go off my rocker."** Don smiled and said, **"That's exactly what I said 20 years ago."** Then he said something else that really made her think: **"You're trying to fit God into your life. Instead you should be trying to make your life revolve around God."** The woman left the restaurant in turmoil. Begin each morning with prayer? Begin each morning with 15minutes of prayer? Absolutely out of the question! Yet, the next morning she found herself doing exactly that. And she's been doing it ever since. This woman is the first to admit that it has not always been easy. There have been mornings when she was filled with great peace and joy. But there have been other mornings when she was filled with nothing but weariness. And it was on these weary mornings that she remembered something else that her marketing consultant said. **"There will be times when your mind just won't go into God's sanctuary. That's when you spend your hour in God's waiting room. Still, you're there, and God appreciates your struggle to stay there."** Today's gospel reminds us of the need of combining work with prayer.

Today's Gospel is a story about two **EXTREMISTS** - Martha and Mary. Very little is said, but if we read between the lines, we can paint a pretty good picture of these two women. **MARTHA is busy and anxious.** She's the type of woman who always needs to be busy and doing things. No wonder Jesus became a friend with her brother Lazarus and frequently visited their home! Martha knew how to cook; she kept a perfect home. She knew how to keep a guest well-fed and happy. Martha was always busy. There was always so much to do.

MARY was the thoughtful type. She stayed in the background. She wanted to think things through, to absorb all she could from the presence of the Lord. Martha's busy-ness probably bothered her, "Why is my sister Martha always so busy with things that don't really matter? When will she learn to look beyond her pots and pans and paintbrushes and that constant cup of tea she always makes for Him? How can I stop her fussing and make her sit down and just listen?"

MARY'S way troubled MARTHA too: "Why can't she just accept Jesus as He is and wait on Him? He'll show us His mystery in His own good time. Right now, He's probably hungry and just wants to rest. Why can't my sister just get up and help me with the dishes?"

In our own ways, we'll all extremists. Sometimes we try to spend ourselves in feverish activity, doing a thousand and one things, making lists and thinking that if we get it all done, everything will work out and God will be pleased. At other times, we come to a complete halt and decide to just sit and think and pray. We want NO DISTRACTIONS from our family and friends. We want time for God and for ourselves.

So which one is right? MARTHA or MARY? The answer is they both are. We can't change who we are. And as the Lord loved both MARTHA and MARY, so the Lord loves each one of us. But we do need to learn a little from each of them. We need to be busy sometimes, doing the things that need to get done, noticing the needs of others. But we also need to be quiet sometimes, taking time to actually pray, to actually be quiet with the Lord. Each of us tends to be sometimes a MARTHA and sometimes a MARY. Maybe this week we might consider letting them join forces in showing us the value of both approaches to God and life. Those of us who are always BUSY might learn to slow down a little. And those of us who sit totally quiet might learn to attach some actions to our Faith and life. We need to work and we need to pray.

And never forget....GOD IS GOOD...ALL THE TIME!

God bless you!

17th Sunday in Ordinary Time - "C"

25 July 2010

FIRST READING: Genesis 18:20-32
PSALM: Psalm 138:1-3, 6-8
SECOND READING: Colossians 2:12-14
GOSPEL: Luke 11:1-13

Sodom and Gomorrah could have been spared if only there had been a few more good people in them.

Another great week in Paradise. We locals are so fortunate to be here. People are paying big bucks to come to Laughlin for a few days, and we get to be here almost every day! I'm usually very lucky on slots and raffles, so I wasn't really too surprised when I got a call this week from Our Lady of Wisdom Church in Las Vegas telling me that I was one of their raffle winners. I had only bought a few chances. I asked what I had won figuring it would be a lot of money, but they said they had added a few prizes, so even though I didn't win a big money prize, I would be happy with what I had won. I asked what that might be, and they told me that I was the lucky winner of a brand new lawnmower! **Oh great, I don't even have a lawn!**

I found a new drink at Walgreen's called FUZE. It's an anti-oxydent flavored water and several of the flavors have no calories at all. It has a great taste. It was $2 a bottle, but was on sale for $1 a bottle, and I found a coupon good for $.50 a bottle, so I stocked up on it last week.....**and Eddie drank most of it.** So I stocked up again this week, and explained that he should leave some for me. He calmly explained that that was not how it works. He said, **"I'm a drinker, you're a buyer. Let's keep it that way!"** Welcome to my world!

I'm blessed with many really great friends. One of my friends, Brad, is a comedian who lives in Missouri. We don't get to see each other much, but we love to banter on Facebook when we get time.

Brad would post a comment, and I'd comment back on it. Here are some of the thoughts we shared this week, trying to outdo each other in fun:

We have enough youth, how about a Fountain of Smart?

What happens if you're scared half to death twice?

I'd kill for a Nobel Peace Prize.

Do you like cats? I do too. Let's exchange recipes.

Change is inevitable except from a vending machine.

The difference between knowledge and wisdom...it is knowledge to know that a tomato is a fruit. It is wisdom to know not to put a tomato in a fruit salad.

One way to look really thin is to hang out with fat people

There are three types of people: those who can count and those who can't.

Polynesia - memory loss in parrots.

Never hit a man with glasses...use a baseball bat instead.

The sole purpose of a child's middle name is to let him know when he is really in trouble.

Since light travels faster than sound, isn't that why some people appear bright until you hear them speak?

Before getting into an argument, walk a mile in the other person's shoes. That way you're a mile ahead of him and he has no shoes.

After we finished, some stranger commented online **"You guys are fun!"**

After messaging with Brad, I usually end up smiling and laughing. It's almost like walking and talking with him in person. I thought of that feeling this week as I read over today's **FIRST READING** from the **BOOK OF GENESIS.** Abraham and God walked and talked together like two really good friends. I thought I would say a few words about that First Reading today.

1. ABRAHAM and GOD walk and talk as two good friends would. You can almost see them together. Abraham and God had a close relationship. And there's something very impressive about ABRAHAM telling GOD how to be GOD! **("FAR BE IT FROM YOU TO DO SUCH A THING! SHOULD NOT THE JUDGE OF THE WORLD ACT WITH JUSTICE?").** I hope that all of us would feel close enough to God to speak honestly with Him. **That, in essence, is what prayer is: SPEAKING HONESTLY WITH GOD AND LISTENING TO HIM WHEN HE REPLIES.** Sure, sometimes we do it with more formality and use precise words, but most of the time we pray really well when we just have a good honest heart-to-heart friendly conversation with God.

2. The value of a **FEW GOOD PEOPLE** is **INCREDIBLE!** Abraham bargains with God to save Sodom. Starting with 50 good people, Abraham bargains with God for the life of the city of Sodom. And each time Abraham lowers the number (50-45-40-30-20-10), God agrees He would not destroy the city because of the presence of those few good people. Ultimately, God agrees that He would not destroy the city if ONLY TEN GOOD PEOPLE could be found there. In a city of thousands, **TEN GOOD PEOPLE** would bring about salvation for themselves and for their whole city! Think about that in some current and local terms:

If one or two more people really were honest in the place where they work, wouldn't it be easier for the whole office or business to be honest?

If one or two more people really taught their children the difference between right and wrong, wouldn't it be easier for those children to grow up and act rightly, and maybe even influence the people around them to do so too?

If one or two more politicians locally and nationally acted with honesty and integrity, wouldn't it make government better for all of us?

If one or two more couples were really faithful to one another in their marriages, realizing that love sometimes means real effort, wouldn't it strengthen marriage and family within our society?

If one or two more people really made the effort to make Sunday Mass a priority, wouldn't that be a good example to the rest of their family and maybe to their neighbors? If parents don't think it's important enough to teach that to their children, that's about as sad as it gets.

The list could go on and on. The point is that YOUR EXAMPLE and the EXAMPLE OF YOUR FAMILY might be just the ONE MORE EXAMPLE needed to save someone from destruction.

REMEMBER THIS: THE CITY OF SODOM WOULD STILL BE STANDING TODAY IF ONLY 10 GOOD PEOPLE HAD BEEN FOUND THERE. You might very well be the ONE MORE PERSON needed to make the difference in someone's salvation or destruction. **You just never know how important you could be.**

God bless you!

18th Sunday in Ordinary Time - "C"

1 August 2010

FIRST READING: Ecclesiastes 1:2, 2:21-23
PSALM: Psalm 90:3-6, 12-14, 17
SECOND READING: Colossians 3:1-5, 9-11
GOSPEL: Luke 12:13-21

This sermon was preached at St. Francis of Assisi Parish in Henderson, Nevada, during my brief tenure there as Temporary Administrator.

Where is our treasure? It's only secure if we are rich in what matters to God.

I love late night conversations, just sitting around and talking. A few weeks ago, I was having dinner at the Peppermill on the Strip in Vegas at about 2:00 AM with some good friends. We got to talking about what our parents did to punish us if we did something wrong as kids. One guy spoke about his parents spanking him, another talked about being sent to his room. When they asked me, I at first tried to explain that I had never done anything wrong as a kid, but they didn't buy that! So I explained that if I did anything really bad, my Mom would throw the parrot at me. One guy choked on his dinner while the others asked me to explain. When I didn't do something that my Mom had asked, she would calmly get a big wooden yardstick, go to the parrot's cage, and the parrot would climb onto the yardstick. She would then hurl the parrot at me and he would land on me with his claws outstretched. This was particularly effective if I didn't want to get out of bed on time for school. There I would be bouncing around in bed trying to unattach the parrot's claws from me! I can still remember my Mom saying: **"Don't make me get the parrot!"**

Another of our late night conversations involved movies. If you were to ask me what kind of movies I really like, you would probably be surprised to find that I like really fast car chases and narrow escapes, I like burning buildings. Of course I also like really funny comedies where people don't get hurt, but laugh a lot and have stupid things happen to them. I just don't like to have to think a lot when I go to the movies. I was once interviewed and asked what my favorite movie was that year, and my response was **THE PUNISHER**. Sure surprised the interviewer! And now you get the idea of my movie tastes.

Things would have been different if I had been living back in the 1500's. But I still would have found some form of entertainment. In fact, even teens in the 1500's would have found some forms of entertainment along with their parents and families. They would have found it in a place you might not now expect. **They would have found it at the parish church!** Back in the late 15th century, about 500 years ago, there were no movies to go to and see. But there were some other forms of entertainment. One of the most popular back then was something called the **MORALITY PLAY**. These were written to convey a message, but they were acted out....sometimes even on the church steps....to entertain the people as well as to make them think. Probably the single most famous morality play written in English is a play called **EVERYMAN**. I suspect that if it were written today, it would have to be politically correct and given the title **EVERYPERSON**. But the original title is **EVERYMAN,** and so it shall always be. **I may not be politically correct, but I am historically accurate!**

It's a hot summer day, here in the 1500's in ye old shire of Henderson, let me take you back for a few moments and mentally out onto the church steps (there was no air-conditioning in those days!) where the action is now commencing.....

Morality plays were extremely straightforward. No hidden meanings here! **EVERYMAN** is the main character and **EVERYMAN** is precisely what his name implies. He is every man (and every woman too!). In the play, **EVERYMAN** is called by **DEATH** (a dark and shadowy character) to report to the end of his life. And

EVERYMAN knows that he must go. So he starts heading along the road to meet his destiny and along the way he encounters many of his old friends. He meets them and tries to really like ones with a lot of **SENSELESS VIOLENCE** or **STUPID SLAPSTICK COMEDY**. I don't usually go to the movies because I want to think! I like helicopters being blown up, Ipersuade them to accompany him when he meets his death. And one by one, his friends leave him to journey alone. You can see them coming up to **EVERYMAN** one at a time:

EVERYMAN meets his friend **STRENGTH**, but strength cannot go with him to death.

EVERYMAN meets his friend **BEAUTY**, but beauty cannot go with him to death.

EVERYMAN meets his friend **KINDRED**, but even his kin cannot go with him to death.

EVERYMAN meets his friends, his **FIVE-SENSES**, and **KNOWLEDGE**, and **FELLOWSHIP**, but none of them can go with him to death.

EVERYMAN meets his friend **WORLDLY GOODS**, a friend with whom he has spent a lot of time in life, but worldly goods cannot accompany him to death.

Finally, **EVERYMAN** meets his friend **GOOD DEEDS**, and Good Deeds says that of course, he will accompany **EVERYMAN** to meet his destiny.

And so the play ends with these lines:

They all at last do **EVERYMAN** forsake
Save his **GOOD DEEDS**, there doth he take.
But beware, and they be small
Before God, he hath no help at all.
None excuse may be there for **EVERYMAN**:
Alas, how shall he do then?
For after death amends may no man make,
For then mercy and pity do him forsake.
If his reckoning be not clear when he do come,
God will say Ite maledicti in ignem aeternum.
And he that hath his account whole and sound
High in heaven he shall be crowned
Unto which place God bring us all thither
That we may live body and soul together
Thereto help the Trinity,
Amen, say ye, for Saint Charity!

Thus endeth this moral play of **EVERYMAN**.

And strangely enough, **EVERYMAN** reflects the message straight from today's Gospel. We all need to be rich in what matters to God. It is still not what we have but what we do for others with what we have that makes all the difference. **We all need to be rich in what matters to God.**

And thus endeth this sermon. Amen.

God bless you!

19th Sunday in Ordinary Time - "C"

8 August 2010

FIRST READING: Wisdom 18:6-9
PSALM: Psalm 33:1, 12, 18-22
SECOND READING: Hebrews 11:1-2, 8-19
GOSPEL: Luke 12:32-48

Faith is many things to many people, but it always leads us to God!

Another beautiful week in Paradise! And **Good Vibrations** are in town at the Riverside, so I'm singing a lot of my favorite **Beach Boy** tunes. As far back as I can remember, the Beach Boys' surfing songs have always been my favorite music of summer!

This week, my friend Drake (yeah, that's his stage name) called. He has been looking to buy a house in Las Vegas. He found one online last Friday, talked to me about it online on Sunday for an hour or so, and sent me up to see it on Tuesday. It's huge! 7000 square feet, a 7 car garage, 5 bedrooms (each with its own bathroom), a 25 foot high stone fireplace, a private laundry room just for the master bedroom, a ten-person hot tub, and a view of the Las Vegas Strip from the South Pointe in the South to Fremont Street in the North. He's getting a great deal on it, and he decided to buy it. So now I can honestly say that I actually visited his house before he did. When I was there, he called me and asked me to tell him my first thoughts on seeing it. All I could say was **"Drake, it's big, really big!"**

Did the month of July seem to go by particularly fast for you this year? Do you feel as though you missed something because the month was over before you even knew it had begun? Well, I was just reading a list of celebrations that occurred in the month of July and I really feel that I missed out on quite a number of them. After all, July was NATIONAL BAKED BEANS MONTH as well as NATIONAL ICE CREAM MONTH, and NATIONAL ANTI-BOREDOM MONTH and NATIONAL HITCHHIKING MONTH.

And several days in July had particularly interesting designations:

July 3 was AIR-CONDITIONING APPRECIATION DAY
July 6 was NATIONAL FRIED CHICKEN DAY
July 7 was NATIONAL STRAWBERRY SUNDAE DAY
July 10 was DON'T STEP ON A BEE DAY
July 11 was NATIONAL CHEER UP THE LONELY DAY
July 12 was NATIONAL PECAN PIE DAY
July 14 was NATIONAL NUDE DAY

July 16 was INTERNATIONAL JUGGLING DAY
July 28 was NATIONAL MILK CHOCOLATE DAY

And now we're already into August, and there is so much to celebrate in so little time! After all, AUGUST is NATIONAL ADMIT YOU'RE HAPPY MONTH as well as NATIONAL GET ACQUAINTED WITH NEW ZEALAND KIWI FRUIT MONTH. And several days in AUGUST have particularly interesting designations:

August 1 was NATIONAL KID'S DAY
August 3 was FRIENDSHIP DAY
August 7 was NATIONAL MUSTARD DAY
August 8 (today) is ADMIT YOU'RE HAPPY DAY
August 8 is also NATIONAL SNEAK SOME ZUCCHINI ONTO YOUR NEIGHBOR'S PORCH NIGHT
August 13 is INTERNATIONAL LEFT-HANDER'S DAY
August 16 is NATIONAL WATERMELON DAY
August 29 is MORE HERBS, LESS SALT DAY
August 31 is LOVE LITIGATING LAWYERS DAY

So much to celebrate.....and so little time! Well, even though many of us missed out on the big July celebrations and some of the August celebrations , our readings today might very well make this 2nd Sunday of August **WORLDWIDE FAITH DAY**. Today's First Reading speaks of the faith involved in serving the Lord consistently, and persevering in faithfulness. But today's

Second Reading from the Letter to the Hebrews is the most eloquent when it speaks of the great faith of Abraham, Isaac and Jacob, as well as their wives and descendants down through the ages. It is a good day for us to think and consider the place of FAITH in our lives.

Faith can be defined as the realization of what is hoped for and the evidence of things not yet seen.

To help us celebrate **WORLDWIDE FAITH DAY**, let me just pass along a few beautiful and memorable thoughts on FAITH that I have seen and liked throughout the years:

FAITH is:
- remembering that I am indispensable to God even when I sometimes feel I only clutter up the landscape.

- doing the right thing regardless of the consequences, knowing that God will turn the ultimate effect of my efforts to good.

- expecting God to accomplish miracles through insignificant little me, even when I only bring my five loaves and two fish.

- recognizing that God is the Lord of all time, even when my idea of timing doesn't quite agree with His.

- confidence that God is acting for my highest good when He answers a resounding "NO" to some of my prayers.

- refusing to feel guilty over past-confessed and forgiven sins, when God the Judge has graciously declared me pardoned.

- realizing that God is the God of RIGHT NOW, carrying out His purposes in every seemingly tedious, dull, stupid, boring, empty minute of my life.

- the conviction that GOD, THE PROMISER, ALWAYS KEEPS HIS PROMISES!

Today really is **WORLDWIDE FAITH DAY** for us! Don't miss out on celebrating it!

There are some things in life that we would never get through without our Faith. It is because of the gift of our Catholic Faith that we gather here every Sunday for Mass so that we can draw strength from our Faith to sustain us throughout the week, because we never know what the week is going to throw at us. May we always be grateful to God for this wonderful gift of Faith, and may we know that God will always keep His promises to us. In short, may we be as faithful to God as we know God has shown Himself to be to us. If we can try to do that, our

Faith can accomplish great things in our lives and in the life of the world.

God bless you!

Eddie, Charlie, Andy and Michael at the Magic Castle in Hollywood!

Assumption of the Blessed Virgin Mary

15 August 2010

FIRST READING: Revelation 11:19; 12:1-6, 10
PSALM: Psalm 45:10-12, 16
SECOND READING: 1 Corinthians 15: 20-27
GOSPEL: Luke 1: 39-56

Mary goes ahead of us as our Mother and as a Model of discipleship.

What a strange week in Paradise....well, actually, not in Paradise completely. I'm sure you've all heard the saying **"If you want to make God laugh, tell Him your plans."** Well, I had a chance to see that in action this week. After being sick on Monday and Tuesday, I decided to make the drive to Vegas on Tuesday evening. I was using a free night at a hotel and I didn't want to miss it. Well, I made it there, but by midnight I was in terrific pain. Knew I couldn't drive, so I called my friend Paul and said, **"Can you take me to the emergency room?"** He came right away, and off we went to UMC's emergency room. I've never been to a city hospital emergency room at midnight. **It's a scary place!** To make a very long story short, they gave me morphine. I've never had morphine....I don't usually even take aspirin! I'm not sure it got rid of the pain, but after the shot I didn't care!

Within a few hours, I had a Cat Scan, X-Rays, Ultra Sound, and a gallon of blood taken from me. Apparently my blood pressure had skyrocketed to 205/90...which really scared the docs. They found a few other things wrong with me, but I'm expected to survive with the help of some blood pressure meds, etc. And they said I would know when the kidney stone passes. **That just sounds ominous!** Two of the funniest scenes of the night were my friend Paul sitting with me in the emergency room cubicle trying to keep me from being scared. Paul's in a major Las Vegas show and even has a fan club. I'm sure all his fans think he has this really fabulous life....and here he is at 3:30 AM sitting next to an older priest in an emergency room. And my nurse the next day was a real sweet girl named Mary Rose. She saw I was from Laughlin so she asked me about our town. Of course, I couldn't pass up the opportunity to tell her about Paradise! She came back several times to ask me more, and finally asked me: **"Do you work for the Laughlin Visitors Bureau?"** When I told her **"No"**, she asked me what I did in Laughlin so I told her I was the Catholic priest here. She stopped, looked at me, and said **"Why didn't you tell me? I would have been nice to you!"** I thought she had been pretty nice anyway. **So Paradise even got a plug from a priest on morphine in Vegas one night this week!** I love this place! Had lunch with Father Peter this week when I got home and he looked at me and told me to take it easy, **"You're not 40 anymore!"** he said. And then he quoted an old Polish saying which I can't remember in Polish but in English it comes out as: **"Getting old is no laughing matter!"**

This weekend we celebrate our 18th anniversary here in Laughlin. We were established on August 15, 1992, and on August 16, 1992, Father John McShane celebrated the first Catholic Masses of our newly-formed Mission of St. John the Baptist in the Hemingway Harbor Room at the old Gold River Gambling Hall at 8:00 AM and 10:00 AM. The total attendance for the two Masses was 285 people. Bishop Daniel Walsh spoke at the Masses about why the name St. John the Baptist was chosen for the mission. Because of our location on the Colorado River and because **"John's role in life was to point out Jesus' presence....In Laughlin, we want the community of faith to point out Jesus...The purpose of starting a church in a community is to help people who believe in Jesus keep their eyes on Jesus."** In November, 1992, I visited Father John and offered Mass here during the 4th month of our existence. I feel as though I've been here from the very beginning. And I visited here to help out under each Administrator who has been here. I've been Administrator here since July 1, 2008, and as of this month, I have been here longer than 3 of my predecessors: Father (now Monsignor) Kevin McAuliffe,

Father Peter Romeo, and Father Ray Schultz. To achieve the record of longevity in Laughlin, all I have to do now is beat out the records of two of my predecessors: Father John McShane who was here for 4 years, and Father Frank Yncierto who was here for 7 years. **Just so you know, I like challenges so I'm betting I win.**

Every priest who has been here at St. John the Baptist has added something of his own style and gifts to this wonderful parish. But we could only do it because of the faith and perseverance of our loyal parishioners, past and present, and our awesome visitors over the years. We're here because of you, and we're here for you. For the past 18 years, we have kept our focus on helping people to keep their eyes on Jesus.

We gather here today as we have gathered at St. John the Baptist for the past 18 years to pray together as a Catholic Family of Faith. We honor our Catholic belief that Mary was assumed into heaven by the power of God when her earthly life was completed. And we pray that when we have faithfully completed our earthly lives, we too will join Mary in the eternal happiness of heaven. Bishop Walsh's message to us that very first Sunday 18 years ago still rings true: The beautiful Colorado River still flows as a reminder to us of Jesus' Presence in our community. We need to keep our eyes on Jesus. And be grateful that He keeps His eyes on us.

God Bless you!

Charlie and Andy and the Armadillo!

21st Sunday in Ordinary Time - "C"

22 August 2010

FIRST READING: Isaiah 66:18-21
PSALM: Psalm 117:1-2
SECOND READING: Hebrews 12:5-7, 11-13
GOSPEL: Luke 13:22-30

"When life gives you lemons, make chocolate chip cookies and an ice cream soda...and let them wonder how you did it!" (Father Charlie)

So, an interesting week in Paradise! On Thursday, the air-conditioner at the rectory died a painful death, and can't be repaired until Monday or Tuesday. I toughed it out in the house at 105 degrees on Thursday night. But on Friday, I was able to rent a room at the Riverside. So for this weekend, I am pretending to be on vacation...sleeping in a hotel room, eating breakfast overlooking the river, and being one of Laughlin's amazing tourists! I love this place!

Earlier this week, I really was on vacation! I took two and a half days off and went to Vegas for a 60 hour Magic Marathon! Met up with two friends from Wyoming and it was **3 Guys, 3 Nights, 8 Shows**! Got to bed most mornings at about 3AM, saw the best magic shows in

Vegas, and got to hang out with the magicians after each show. Even had a two-hour lunch one day with **Murray SawChuck**, one of the magicians currently on America's Got Talent. Murray, by the way, is the only contestant on AGT who has been to Mass with us here in Laughlin, so besides being an awesome magician, he's getting my vote because of our friendship and his connection with Laughlin. To help you remember him, Murray is the **"guy with the freaky hair!"**

Besides getting no sleep, we also ate at unusual times. Had dinner one night at 2:00 AM, and even celebrated what would have been Elvis Presley's 33rd anniversary of death on Monday by eating **DEEP-FRIED TWINKIES**....and they were darn good! Both guys with me for the Magic Marathon were much younger than I am, so they got proofed at every bar and restaurant and club and casino we went to. I never got proofed at all! Although when I asked about it, one pretty cocktail server told me, **"I'm thinking about it"** but then she never proofed me!

At the end of the 60 hours, we all agreed - That was fun! We need to do it again!

We do have a lot of fun in life, and that's a good thing. One of the worst advertisements for Christianity and our Catholic Faith is people who claim to be followers of Jesus but who see nothing but evil and gloom in the world. We've all run into them. They never smile, they look like they've been chomping on lemons, and they can't seem to say anything good about the world, life, their neighbors, etc. They are unhappy, and it seems that they want to make everyone else around them unhappy too. My advice is to stay as far away from such people as you possibly can! At the end of the world, they sure are going to be surprised at the people God is letting into His eternal Kingdom! When today's Gospel speaks of all the people coming together in God's Kingdom from the East and the West, and from the North and the South, some who think they are the only ones worthy to be chosen are going to be surprised! I love that line in today's Gospel: **"Some are last who will be first, and some are first who will be last."** It offers so much hope to so many of us!

On Thursday of this week, we commemorate the 100th birthday of Mother Teresa of Calcutta. Now she is definitely a person who knows about the mercy and love of God, and who sees so much goodness and hope in the world. I've printed a number of quotations from her in today's bulletin and I hope you will take the time to read them and think about them. I think it's fitting that we hear a few of them right now:

"Spread love everywhere you go. Let no one ever come to you without leaving happier."

"Good works are links that form a chain of love."

"I am a little pencil in the hand of a writing God who is sending a love letter to the world."

"Peace begins with a smile."

"We can do no great things, only small things with great love."

And Mother Teresa was a realist. One of my favorite things she ever said is:

"I know God will not give me anything I can't handle. I just wish that He didn't trust me so much." I think there are times when we can all agree with that thought.

I'd just like to add one thing. It's not from Mother Teresa, but I picked it up from a friend. You've all heard the saying, **"When life gives you lemons, make lemonade"**, well, my version of that would be: **"When life gives you lemons, make chocolate chip cookies and an ice cream soda...and let them wonder how you did it!"**

God bless you!

Spandy Andy, Charlie, and Destiny Shami

22nd Sunday in Ordinary Time - "C"

29 August 2010

FIRST READING: Sirach 3:17-18, 20, 28-29
PSALM: Psalm 68:4-7, 10-11
SECOND READING: Hebrews 12:18-19, 22-24
GOSPEL: Luke 14:1, 7-14

He's going to make it! I know he is!

What a crazy week here in Paradise! Last weekend, I ended up living at the Riverside because the air-conditioning system at the rectory died. It was fixed this week, and I got to enjoy it on Thursday night. Then we had that huge electrical storm on Friday night, and it blew out the air-conditioning system again! I think God is trying to tell me something! So unless it can be fixed today, I'm back to being a tourist staying in a hotel!

Years ago, when I really was a tourist in Nevada, I got to know a guy out here named Steve. Steve got into trouble with the law over 20 years ago. He ended up being sent to the Nevada State Prison System, and has been incarcerated in several locations around the state. For years, he was up in Ely, Nevada, 4 hours North of Las Vegas. And each summer, I'd drive up to Ely to spend 6 hours with him in a bare visiting room with a couple of vending machines so we could get sodas and bags of chips. In recent years, he was moved to Indian Springs, only 45 minutes outside of Las Vegas, and we'd follow the same routine when I was out in Vegas. Well, he got released just before I moved out here after being in prison for 18 years and 7 months. He's now 42 and had been in prison for almost half his lifetime. I got to spend a lot of time with him during the first week he was released and it was like being out with Rip Van Winkle! Just imagine what it would be like to leave the world in 1989, and then come back again in 2007! Everything was so different!

Steve used to run a betting pool in prison. The other inmates would bet postage stamps on the outcome of football/basketball games. In a good month, Steve would have a few hundred postage stamps. He'd mail them to a priest in NJ who would buy them for his parish and then put the money on his books so Steve could buy some snacks or clothing. **Yeah, I was that priest.** One day Pat (my secretary in NJ) asked me how come we never had stamps on sheets, but only these piles of individual stamps! I finally had to tell her the story....and after that she never wanted to lick any more of the stamps I had bought!

I asked Steve what was the biggest surprise so far in the couple of days after he had gotten out of prison. He said he went into the bathroom of a hotel when the bus dropped him off in Las Vegas. He was at the toilet. And couldn't find the handle to flush it! Kept looking all around for it and moving his hands over it, and finally stepped away and it flushed. Then he went to the sink to wash his hands, and there were no faucets. So he figured it might be like the urinal, and he moved his hands all over it, and sure enough the water came on!

He's going to make it. He got a driver's license while I was there, and moved into a halfway house, and even got a job moving furniture. He enrolled in school and is going to finish up his college degree, and I took him out for his first steak dinner in almost 20 years. In these past years of freedom, he's gotten his own apartment, got a permanent job, and is really making a great new start in his life. It's as if he is seeing everything for the first time! Everything is new, everything is exciting to him.

Next weekend is Labor Day, the unofficial end of summer, the unofficial start of the new school year around our country, the time when we all restart our routines and rebuild our habits. Maybe we can learn something from Steve and see that God gives us all new opportunities, new beginnings. Things don't have to be just the same old routine, we can change, we can make things better for ourselves and for those around us.

Today's Gospel reminds us to approach God with humility, to recognize that all that we have comes to us from Him. If we've been asleep, or careless, or even sinful, we can still come back to God and make a new beginning. And maybe that's a really good lesson for us as Labor Day weekend approaches. We can all make a new beginning!

And make sure that being here is part of your weekly habits and routines in this new beginning. This actually is the most important part of our week. We belong at Mass on Sundays. **It's what Catholics do.** And it will help each of us to be strong and courageous in the other new beginnings of our lives. It is humbling to recognize that we can't do it alone....we need God and we need each other. But God's promise is sure: **"Everyone who exalts himself will be humbled, but the one who humbles himself will be exalted."**

God bless you!

John Rotellini, David Goldrake, and Charlie

23rd Sunday in Ordinary Time - "C"

5 September 2010

FIRST READING: Wisdom 9:13-18
PSALM: Psalm 90:3-6, 12-17
SECOND READING: Philemon 9-10, 12-17
GOSPEL: Luke 14: 25-33

This sermon was preached at St. Francis of Assist Parish in Henderson, Nevada, on this date during my brief tenure as Temporary Administrator. You may notice that I have **"recycled"** some of today's sermon in Henderson from my sermon last weekend in Laughlin. Yes, we priests and deacons sometimes get more than one use from some sermon materials! I'll bet you, Gentle Reader, suspected that!

> *There's nothing in life that is worthwhile that doesn't cost you something.*

A few weeks ago, I was on vacation! I took two and a half days off and went to Vegas for a **60 hour Magic Marathon**! Met up with two friends from Wyoming and it was **3 Guys, 3 Nights, 8 Shows**! Got to bed most mornings at about **3AM**, saw the best magic shows in Vegas, and got to hang out with the magicians after each show. Besides getting no sleep, we also ate at unusual times. Had dinner one night at 2:00 AM, and even celebrated one of Elvis Presley's favorite foods by eating **DEEP-FRIED TWINKIES**....and they were darn good! Both guys with me for the Magic Marathon are much younger than I am, so they got proofed at every bar and restaurant and club and casino we went to. I never got proofed at all! Although when I asked about it, one pretty cocktail server told me, **"I'm thinking about it"** but then she never proofed me!

At the end of the 60 hours, we all agreed - That was fun! We need to do it again!

We do have a lot of fun in life, and that's a good thing. One of the worst advertisements for Christianity and our Catholic Faith is people who claim to be followers of Jesus but who see nothing but evil and gloom in the world. We've all run into them. They never smile, they look like they've been chomping on lemons, and they can't seem to say anything good about the world, life, their neighbors, etc. They are unhappy, and it seems that they want to make everyone else around them unhappy too. My advice is to stay as far away from such people as you possibly can! At the end of the world, they sure are going to be surprised at the people God is letting into His eternal Kingdom! A few weeks ago, the Sunday Gospel spoke of all the people coming together in God's Kingdom from the East and the West, and from the North and the South.

Some who think they are the only ones worthy to be chosen are going to be surprised! I love the line in that Gospel: **"Some are last who will be first, and some are first who will be last."** It offers so much hope to so many of us!

Speaking of hope, some years ago, when I was a tourist in Nevada, I got to know a guy out here named Steve. Steve got into trouble with the law over 20 years ago. He ended up being sent to the Nevada State Prison System, and has been incarcerated in several locations around the state. For years, he was up in Ely, Nevada, 4 hours North of Las Vegas. And each summer, I'd drive up to Ely to spend 6 hours with him in a bare visiting room with a couple of vending machines so we could get soda and a bag a chips. In recent years, he was moved to Indian Springs, only 45 minutes outside of Las Vegas, and we'd follow the same routine when I was out in Vegas. Well, he got released just before I moved out here after being in prison for 18 years and 7 months. He's now 42 and had been in prison for almost half his lifetime. I got to spend a lot of time with him during the first week he was released and it was like being out with Rip Van Winkle! Just imagine what it would be like to leave the world in 1989, and then come back again in 2007! Everything was so different!

Steve used to run a betting pool in prison. The other inmates would bet postage stamps on the outcome of football/basketball games. In a good month, Steve would have a few hundred postage stamps. He'd mail them to a priest in NJ who would buy them for his parish and then put the money on his books so Steve could buy some snacks or clothing. Yeah, I was that priest. One day Pat (my secretary in NJ) asked me how come we never had stamps on sheets, but only these piles of individual stamps! I finally had to tell her the story....and after that she never wanted to lick any more of the stamps I had bought!

He's going to make it. He got a driver's license while I was there, and moved into a halfway house, and even got a job moving furniture. He enrolled in school and is going to finish up his college degree, and I took him out for his first steak dinner in almost 20 years. In these past years of freedom, he's gotten his own apartment, got a permanent job, and is really making a great new start in his life. It's as if he is seeing everything for the first time! Everything is new, everything is exciting to him.

This weekend is Labor Day, the unofficial end of summer, the unofficial start of the new school year around our country, the time when we all restart our routines and rebuild our habits. Maybe we can learn something from Steve and see that God gives us all new opportunities, new beginnings. Things don't have to be just the same old routine, we can change, we can make things better for ourselves and for those around us.

If we've been asleep, or careless, or even sinful, we can still come back to God and make a new beginning. And maybe that's a really good lesson for us on Labor Day weekend. **We can all make a new beginning!**

And make sure that being here is part of your weekly habits and routines in this new beginning. This actually is the most important part of our week. We belong at Mass on Sundays. **It's what Catholics do!** And it will help each of us to be strong and courageous in the other new beginnings of our lives. It is humbling to recognize that we can't do it alone....we need God and we need each other.

No matter who we are or where we are, one thing does remain constant, our lives and lifestyles all cost us something. We all want to know what our actions are going to cost. All of us are careful when it comes to figuring out what something will cost us in terms of money, or in time, or in reputation. We might not always say it out loud, but it's a background question throughout our lives: **WHAT WILL THIS COST ME?** And it is not a **BAD** question to ask. **Everything costs something.** Telling you about my friends the magicians, or my friend

Steve from the prison, probably costs me some of my quiet reputation. Being a Catholic Christian costs us some of our freedom. It means that we have to learn to treat our possessions and the people in our lives in a certain way. It means that we have to be willing to give God the worship that He deserves as far as we are able. **If our Catholic Faith requires no effort from us than it's worthless.**

We can't be forgiven without repenting for our sins. We can't have our children baptized without actually raising them in our Faith and worship. We can't go off and be married without the blessing of our Church. We can't just sleep in on Sundays or let our children do so and think we are actually being faithful to God. We can't cheat on our income taxes or tell lies at work or deliberately live in sin or treat others unfairly and still think we can call ourselves good Catholics or Christians.

Without a doubt, it is going to cost you time and effort to be a faithful Catholic. **But there's nothing in life that is worthwhile that doesn't cost you something.** And our Catholic Faith is something worthwhile to profess and to practice.

I am convinced that there is nothing better we can do for ourselves, for our families, for our communities and for our world than to build up our relationship with Almighty God. But it is something for which each one of us has to pay the cost of being a faithful disciple of the Lord. And if what we believe about eternity is true, then it is worth whatever it costs us to do it.

God bless you!

24th Sunday in Ordinary Time - "C"

12 September 2010

FIRST READING: Exodus 32:7-11, 13-14
PSALM: Psalm 51: 3-4, 12-13, 17, 19
SECOND READING: 1 Timothy 1:12-17
GOSPEL: Luke 15:1-32

Perhaps this is the first step in forgiveness for all of us - to pray for the sinner.

September 11th - what a mix of emotions today's date brings to us. Most of us can pinpoint the exact spot where we were when we heard the news of the demented Islamic terrorists smashing two commercial jetliners into the World Trade Center Towers. In fact, many of us had gotten to our TV sets in time to actually see the 2nd plane hit the towers. And then the news reported a third plane crashing into the Pentagon, and a fourth plane went down in Western Pennsylvania, diverted from a target by the efforts of some very brave passengers. **And then for the first time in the history of American aviation, all air traffic was brought to a halt to counter any other planned attacks.** The memories of the towers collapsing, the loss of life, the heroism of the police, fire and medical services - all of these crowd our minds today. **September 11, 2001, changed our lives.** It marked the beginning of the war on terrorism that continues even today in far-off Iraq and Afghanistan, as well as here at home and throughout the world. We come to church today with all of this on our mind, and we sincerely offer our prayers for ourselves and for all those who died in those terrible events as well as for all those whose lives were severely altered by them.

And then we are confronted with today's readings, instructing and pleading with us to be people who can forgive. Moses pleading for his wayward people to be forgiven, St. Paul telling Timothy how deeply he appreciates God forgiving him, and Jesus telling us the Parable of the Prodigal Son in which the boy's father forgives and welcomes the boy home.

The younger son in that story is a really (REALLY!) dislikeable character! First of all, he does something unthinkable - he asks his father for his inheritance before his father dies. Parents, imagine one of your children coming to you and saying out loud: **"You know the money I'm going to get from you when you die?...Well, I want it all now!"** And we think we have family problems! Then, this younger son goes away and wastes the money in a foreign country on a life of dissipation. Even his reason for coming back home is questionable. He doesn't come back home because he loves his father; he comes back home because he is broke and hungry! He still wants to take from his father. He even rehearses a little speech. It is hard for us to feel any sympathy for him at all. And yet, the father not only takes him back, the father actually has been waiting for his return and runs out to greet him! The father wants him back, he belongs to the family no matter what he has done.

You and I tend to put some obstacles in the way of God's love for us. We sometimes think badly, act badly, and are not always very lovable. Sometimes we can be as rude and as insensitive and conniving as that younger son. **And yet, God pursues us relentlessly.** He wants us back even when we don't want Him, or don't want Him for the right reasons.

Notice too that the father in the parable even wants the elder son back, the one who doesn't understand the father's generosity at all. By the way, also notice how the elder brother keeps saying **"YOUR SON"** to his father, but the father keeps saying he is **"YOUR BROTHER."** Even with his seething anger and jealousy, the father wants this son back too.

God is like that loving father, watching the road, looking for all His children to come back home where they belong.

Because of our remembrance of 9/11 and because of today's Gospel, we really have to say a few things about forgiveness:

1. **Forgiveness is not easy.** In fact, it is the single most difficult aspect of Catholic Christianity to understand and to practice. But God wants us always to be ready to forgive. We need to pray for those who sin against God and against us. We need to pray and work that they see the evil that they do and want to stop doing it. **Perhaps this is the first step in forgiveness for all of us - to pray for the sinner.**

2. **We all need to be forgiven.** Not one of us is free from sin. That younger son in today's Gospel could be any one of us, going off and wasting our lives. We need to go to God and sincerely ask His forgiveness for our own sins. We need to pray that we see the evil that we do, and that we stop doing it. **When we pray for sinners, we need to include ourselves.** That, by the way, is one of the reasons why we Catholics come to Mass each Sunday. We know we need God's help to be forgiven and we pray that those who do not come will change their ways. I've always like the story of the man who said he wouldn't come to church because there are so many hypocrites there. And the preacher told him, that's okay, **"There's always room for one more!"**

3. **Forgiveness does not mean that the offense never happened.** The United States was really brutally attacked on 9/11/01. Innocent people really died. The younger son in today's Gospel really wasted his inheritance. Praying and working for forgiveness does not mean that we forget the evil that was done.

4. **Forgiveness does not mean that we condone or allow evil to continue.** Even God cannot forgive a sinner who does not repent of his evil. We must never approve of evil or condone it or allow it to exist when we can stop it. That's why we have to keep up the pressure on the terrorists and dismantle their organizations. That's why we need to check our own behavior when we stray from our Catholic Faith and it's teachings.

When we pray the Lord's Prayer later in this Mass, think about what we are asking God when we say: **FORGIVE US OUR TRESPASSES AS WE FORGIVE THOSE WHO TRESPASS AGAINST US.** Do we really understand what we are asking God to do? Do we really want God to do that? Do we really want God to treat us the way we treat those around us?

Sometimes it's worthwhile to see where we stand in a parable. Are we like the younger son who has strayed and wants to come back home? Are we like the older son who feels he has never strayed, but who now feels unrewarded by his father? Are we like the father, who reaches out to both of his sons with love and understanding and forgiveness? I think that in the course of our lives, we can sometimes be like each of them.

Let me just end with a story:

Two little brothers, Harry and James, had finished supper and were playing. Somehow, Harry hit James with a stick. Tears and bitter words followed. Even as their mother prepared them for bed, they were still at it. Finally, their mother said: **"Now boys, what would happen if either of you died tonight and you never had the opportunity again for forgiving one another?"** James (who had been the one hit) spoke up: **"Well, OK, I'll forgive him tonight.....but if we're both alive in the morning, he'd better look out!"** Hopefully, the forgiveness we practice and seek will be more lasting than that!

May God bless us to know and appreciate His forgiveness and to imitate it throughout our lives!

God bless you!

Father John McShane (First Priest assigned to Laughlin)
and Father Charlie Urnick (Current Priest assigned to
Laughlin) enjoying the St. John the Baptist Catholic
Church Christmas Party!

25th Sunday in Ordinary Time - "C"

19 September 2010

FIRST READING: Amos 8:4-7
PSALM: Psalm 113:1-2, 4-8
SECOND READING: 1 Timothy 2:1-8
GOSPEL: Luke 16: 1-13

"It's amazing how much can be accomplished when nobody cares who gets the credit." (John Wooden)

Another really awesome week here in Paradise. I know the Pope is over in England for the beatification ceremonies for **Cardinal John Henry Newman**, but I'm sure he's not having as much fun as I am! Last Sunday, our comedy magic show over at the Pioneer raised **$1527** for our local food bank. Really sincere thanks to all who came and had fun with us. Look forward to more events like it in the future. Both of the performers (Spike and Hammer) said they thought the Laughlin audience was one of the most fun audiences they have ever had! I could have told them that!

My brother Michael came home from New York this week and was trying to get me to do some exercises with him. **He still thinks I'm out of shape.** He asked me to do a pull-up, and I laughed as I told him I would gladly do that, but we don't have a pull-up bar.....wouldn't you know he brought one and set it up in the door frame! Darn! They are a lot harder than they look! **Now I have him and Eddie on my case!**

Watched a **FOOD NETWORK** show to get my mind off the pull-up thing, and watched some woman do a recipe for a cocktail sauce that included yogurt, mayonnaise, mustard, and maple syrup. Surprisingly, it sounded pretty good. And I had a peanut butter, banana, and bacon sandwich on Friday night with a friend. Interesting combination, and I heard that Elvis liked it, although I kind of doubt it could be healthy!

Saw a really scary magic show called **PLAYDEAD** up in Vegas on Friday night. Thank goodness I went with some really good friends. It was fun being scared, but it wouldn't have been as much fun if I didn't have someone to grab onto when I screamed! And just before the show, I played a penny slot, and hit a super jackpot! I thought I had won about $30 (which would have been thrilling!), but then I saw the 75 times multiplier and watched it count out over $2000.00 to me! Wow! Was I ever surprised!

So that was my week! And I loved it! And you know, none of it would have happened without some pretty amazing friends. We couldn't have raised the money for the food bank without a lot of really great people supporting the show. I'd never be reminded that I need to exercise without some thoughtful and sarcastic friends and family. I wouldn't see the shows I see or eat the meals I eat or have the conversations I have without some really great people in my life. And we all have people like that in and around our lives. People who are good for us to know, to hang out with, to talk to, to share with. Sometimes they are family members, sometimes they are friends or neighbors; sometimes they are just strangers who cross our pathways. And sometimes they are us. **We are the good people in someone else's life.**

It occurs to me that a lot of times in life, we never find out the full extent of the good we do. We give to a charity, we donate food to the poor, we listen to a friend on the phone, we pray for someone in our neighborhood or family. We probably do a lot of good that never gets us any recognition. Like Timothy in today's second reading, we know that we're supposed to pray, but it is sometimes hard to continue praying when we don't see immediate results for our prayers. And like the servant in today's Gospel, we know we can't serve two masters, but sometimes it is hard to work diligently for God when we seem to be doing it unseen by others. I guess all of us like to get noticed every now and then.

I've always like a quotation attributed to John Wooden.

Now I had absolutely no clue who John Wooden is, but a little reading enlightened me that he is considered one of the greatest college basketball coaches of all time. **His career spanned 27 years at UCLA.** He never screamed or cursed at his players the way some sports idiots do today. But he surely encouraged them to be their best no matter who was watching. I never thought I'd live to see the day that I would be quoting a basketball coach, but I loved his line: **"It's amazing how much can be accomplished when nobody cares who gets the credit."** Think about that line this week. It doesn't matter if you get thanked for the good you do, it doesn't matter if someone erects a plaque with your name on it, it doesn't even matter if you get the credit. **What matters is that you do the good that you're capable of doing.** And you do it precisely because it is good, not because someone is going to give you a gold star or medal. Even if someone else ends up with the credit, so what! **At least the good was done.**

That makes sense in basketball, but it also makes sense in life. Look for the good being done in and around your life, and be sure to put some good into the lives of those around you this week.

"It's amazing how much can be accomplished when nobody cares who gets the credit."

God bless you!

Mike Hammer even helped me to advertise one of my books!

Mike Rayburn came to Laughlin to celebrate my birthday!

26th Sunday in Ordinary Time - "C"

26 September 2010

FIRST READING: Amos 6: 1, 4-7
PSALM: Psalm 146:7-10
SECOND READING: 1 Timothy 6:11-16
GOSPEL: Luke 16: 19-31

"I just couldn't leave Paradise!" (Father Charlie)

What a truly amazing week this has been! Had some friends in from Florida up in Vegas so I got to play tourguide. Stayed out one night with them until 2:30 AM. It's good I don't need much sleep! Here in Paradise, people dropped off homemade chocolate chip cookies, banana nut bread, and an awesome turkey sandwich filled with stuffing and cranberry sauce, so I've been eating really good! Speaking of eating, I attended the **Circle of Roses** dinner on Friday night up in Vegas. It's the big annual fundraiser for the **St. Therese Center**. Besides being a lot of fun for a really good cause, it was also interesting for two other reasons. The men of Chippendales were there and I vowed not to stand anywhere near them in pictures....they would have made me look really bad! And the other reason was that Bishop Pepe was being honored at the dinner for his support of the St. Therese Center, and he was unable to attend. So the diocese called me and asked me to accept the award in place of the bishop and represent the diocese at the dinner. My first thought was **"Gee, there must be no other priests going!"** I've never impersonated a bishop before! And it definitely was the closest I'm ever going to get to being a bishop! Hopefully I did well. Wouldn't mind impersonating him again if needed!

Speaking of Bishop Pepe, I have good news and bad news to share with you this weekend. The bad news is that we won't be seeing Father John down here in Laughlin except on some special occasions. The good news is that Bishop Pepe **accepted my recommendation** that Father John be appointed as Administrator at St. Francis in Henderson, and that I be left as Administrator here at St. John the Baptist in Laughlin. **I'm much more the "country boy" and as I explained to the bishop this summer "my heart is securely tied to Laughlin."** Even the bishop agrees that my heart and body need to be here in Laughlin. You can read my whole letter to the parishioners at St. Francis of Assisi in today's bulletin, and as of Monday, **I am totally and completely here in St. John the Baptist in Laughlin for a long, long time to come.** Hey, it's no surprise. **I just couldn't leave Paradise!** So, I've been able to convince the bishop to appoint Father John as Administrator at St. Francis of Assisi, and I've been able to convince the bishop to leave me here at St. John the Baptist. I wonder what I should ask him for next? Maybe he just likes it when I impersonate him!

Meanwhile, back on the East Coast, this past week marked the big San Gennaro Feast. San Gennaro (St. Januarius) is the patron saint of Naples, and his feast is September 19th. Every year there is a huge 10 day celebration in the Little Italy section of NYC. Streets are blocked off and there is a 10 day orgy of Italian foods and fun. I've only gone to the feast once, but I've never forgotten it! It was an incredible time! There was food everywhere! Zeppoli, Italian pastry, deep fried seafood, pasta, fried mozzarella cheese, nougat candy. The sights and sounds and smells were unbelievable! There were some interesting fund raising booths too: like **drown the clown** (a huge dunk tank) and **shoot the freak** (a paintball competition). The most intriguing one, though, was a huge chair. It was called the **BIG CHAIR**. And for $6.00, you could sit in the **BIG CHAIR** and they would take a Polaroid picture of you. I never did figure out the appeal of the **BIG CHAIR**, but there were people lining up to sit in it. The biggest surprise of the night was the parking fee: **$20 for the first hour, and $40 if you wanted to stay more than an hour!** Had we spent money on the **BIG CHAIR**, we might not have been able to get the car back that night! But a night out with a good friend was worth whatever we ended up paying.

Sometimes it is good to spend our money on ourselves and on our friends. Other times, though, we need to see a bigger picture, bigger even than the **BIG CHAIR**. We need to see those around us who really need our assistance, even when we may at first not notice them. And sometimes the reason we don't notice them is because we just don't pay attention to them.

Today's First Reading from the Prophet Amos, and today's Gospel from St. Luke both speak to us about people who thought of themselves as important...too important to care of the needs of those around themselves. In Amos, we read: **"Woe to the complacent. They are not made ill by the collapse of Joseph."** Their crime is that they did not get upset, they remained calm as their nation deteriorated. In the Gospel, the **RICH MAN** is not punished because he **HARMED** Lazarus, but because he did nothing to help him. In the past, we used to call these things **"sins of omission"**, sins of neglecting to do what should have been done.

This week we need to give some thought to those things in our lives that we have not done, but should have done for those people around us who make up our lives. Those hearts we could have uplifted, but didn't; those needs we could have alleviated, but didn't; those people we could have reached out to, but didn't. All the good that could have become a reality, but didn't.

A medieval philosopher, St. Thomas Aquinas, defined **EVIL** as **"the absence of good where there should be good."** It is possible that our lack of doing good for others around us who are in need is a cause for some of the evil that exists in our world today. Nature abhors a vacuum, and evil easily fills in spaces that good should be filling.

St. Matthew reminds us later in his Gospel that we will all be called to account at the end of the world not for the **WRONGS** we have done so much as for the **GOOD** we have left undone - the naked we have not clothed, the hungry and thirsty we have not satisfied, the poor, sick and imprisoned we have not helped. **The rich man did not hurt Lazarus the beggar, he only failed to help him.** Certainly we are not lacking opportunities in our own lives to help others in need. In the light of Our Lord's words today in the Gospel, can any of us afford to leave them unhelped any longer? This week, try to remember St. Thomas' definition of **EVIL**: It is the absence of good where there should be good. This week, look for any opportunity for doing a good action. **It will give evil less space in which to work!**

God bless you!

27th Sunday in Ordinary Time - "C"

3 October 2010

FIRST READING: Habakkuk 1: 2-3; 2:2-4
PSALM: Psalm 95: 1-2, 6-9
SECOND READING: 2 Timothy 1:6-8, 13-14
GOSPEL: Luke 17: 5-10

And know that CHURCHMAN will be proud of you!

Remember a few weeks ago, I told you about my friend Drake who was looking at a huge house (7100 square feet) up in Vegas? Well, Drake bought the house. Back in the late 1990's, Drake had a magic show here in Laughlin for over a year at the Gold River (now the River Palms). Since he's likely to come down to visit, I figured I should tell you a little more about him.

Drake is a magician who came home to Massachusetts to take care of his Dad who had alzheimer's and had had a stroke. I had never met Drake's Dad until a few summer's ago. I should mention that Drake and his Dad are **Jewish** so I'm kind of the token Catholic in the group. When I was driving up there to meet his Dad for the very first time, Drake thought it would be a good idea to try to prepare his Dad for meeting me by telling him what I did for a living in case I came up wearing my Roman Collar. So the night before I drove up from New Jersey, Drake reminded his Dad that **"Charlie is coming tomorrow."** And he asked his Dad if he knew what Charlie did for a living. His Dad said **"No"**, so Drake told him that **"Charlie is a priest."** Well, his Dad sat up in the bed and said **"What? I'm dying! You've called in the priest!"** So Drake had to reassure him, **"Dad, you're Jewish. If you were dying, I'd be calling in the Rabbi!"** I wonder why people (even some Catholics) think that calling in the priest is like calling in the **Grim Reaper** for a visit?

Well, it turns out that Drake's Dad (whose nickname is "Lucky") and I hit it off real well. We both love Vegas and magic! So we were able to talk about those topics a lot. And even the repetition because of the alzheimer's didn't bother me. I can talk about Vegas and magic for hours, and I don't mind repeating myself!

Well, soon after our first meeting, it was Lucky's 87th birthday, so Drake invited me up to be with him for it because his Dad kept talking about me. And as luck would have it, Drake's sister visited that week. So Drake brought her up to the nursing home to see their Dad. He said they were talking so happily that he decided to leave the two of them together and go out for coffee. When he got back, his sister was hysterically screaming and his Dad was all agitated in the bed. He didn't know what had happened! So he asked his sister **"What happened?"** And through her sobbing and tears, she told him **"Dad is talking crazy, and he's going to die! He told me his priest is coming to see him on his birthday!"** Meanwhile, Lucky looks at Drake and asks **"Isn't Charlie coming, he promised to come for my birthday!"** So once he stopped laughing, Drake had to reassure his sister that their Dad really did know a priest and the priest was coming on Thursday! And we had a really good time on Thursday celebrating his birthday! **Lucky didn't think his Jewish friends would believe I was a priest, so he told them I was his bookie!** He still hasn't lost his sense of humor! And I'm glad that I'm not really the Grim Reaper!

One of my birthdays that I always remember is my 6th birthday. My all-time favorite super-hero was Superman, always fighting for **"Truth, justice and the American way!"** I loved watching Superman on TV and I even wrote him an invitation to my 6th birthday party! (I don't remember how I addressed it, but I did mail it myself!). And then I waited and waited, but he never came to my party. But then I figured he must have been busy fighting the bad guys, so it was okay that he was too busy for my party. **(And I even told him that in my next letter!)**

Whenever I think of Superman, I think about a young guy in my New Jersey parish who several years ago developed a unique greeting for me when he was just a little kid. Every time he saw me at the Sign of Peace at Mass, he would smile, "HIGH FIVE ME", and say **"HI, CHURCHMAN!"** I loved that greeting and always looked forward to it! I've been thinking about it a little this week, and considering what a real **SUPERHERO** named **CHURCHMAN** would be like. So if I really were a superhero named **CHURCHMAN**, here are the results of my thoughts:

I think I'd have a big blue cape with maybe a cross or a steeple on it and that'd be really cool. I'd worry about the spandex, but maybe **CHURCHMAN** could be a Superhero with loose-fitting slacks. And I think **CHURCHMAN** would do some important things. I think he'd hear the Apostles in today's Gospel asking Jesus to **"Increase our Faith"** and he'd show them opportunities to do God's work in the world which would certainly increase their faith. I think he'd remind people that Church is where they have to be on Sundays if they want to be close to God and learn His ways. I think **CHURCHMAN** would work to promote a real respect for all life on this planet, but especially for human life. He'd show people that we can respect life no matter how old or young we are. If we drive, we need to drive carefully. If we speak, we need to speak truthfully. If we work, we need to work conscientiously and not goof off. **CHURCHMAN** would surely work to protect the most innocent and vulnerable members of our society.

CHURCHMAN would also help us to get close to God through prayer. Like St. Francis, **CHURCHMAN** would love all of nature and be known for finding good in as many people as possible. Like Mother Teresa, **CHURCHMAN** would help the poor one at a time and never look for a reward or fame or a pat on the back. Like St. Therese, **CHURCHMAN** would know that Jesus loves people who can smile and radiate happiness even when things are not perfect in their lives. In fact, I think **CHURCHMAN** would call all of the Saints his friends and try to introduce us to all of them throughout the year, kind of like our Catholic Church does with a saint's day every day.

And **CHURCHMAN** would pray, because he would know that even a Superhero is nothing without God. And it is worth all the effort we can muster to stay close to God, to pray and to worship him. After all, **CHURCHMAN** is a Superhero only because of God. And **CHURCHMAN** is a smart-enough Superhero to realize that. I think the Rosary would be among His favorite prayers because of the strength it gives to us.

I know I'm not really **CHURCHMAN**, (even though my brother Michael says that sometimes I think I'm God!) but it was fun thinking about being a Superhero of the Faith. And who knows, maybe I can do a few **CHURCHMAN**-LIKE things in the course of my life. In fact, all of us can do superhero-like things because of our Faith. Just as Jesus said in today's Gospel: **"If you have faith the size of a mustard seed, you would say to this mulberry tree, BE UPROOTED AND PLANTED IN THE SEA, and it would obey you."** I like to think that our faith is a bit larger than a mustard seed, so we really do have super powers for good thanks to God.

This week, look for opportunities to use your powers for good, even when it might take a superhero's effort to do it. Good is always stronger than evil. So faithfully combat evil with your best good efforts! And know that **CHURCHMAN** will be proud of you!

God bless you!

Drake and Father Charlie out at a Celebrity Roast!

Andrew Gill and Father Charlie checking out a Million Dollars!

28th Sunday in Ordinary Time - "C"

10 October 2010

FIRST READING: 2 Kings 5:14-17
PSALM: Psalm 98: 1-4
SECOND READING: 2 Timothy 2:8-13
GOSPEL: Luke 17: 11-19

Someone saw a truth and acted upon it!

Just another awesome week in Paradise! After eating very well here, I got up to my Vegas home and my brother Michael kind of gave me a choice between doing 90 minutes of hard core exercises with him, or going out for a good long walk. Since the exercises would have meant certain death, I chose the walk and lived to tell about it. Then, along with some other priests from the diocese, I was invited to have lunch with Bishop Pepe at his home on Thursday. I asked his secretary about the dress code and she said to come casual. So there I was with about 10 priests in their black shirts and Roman collars, and I was wearing my Las Vegas socks with flames on them, and my new shirt with dollar signs on it. **Apparently "casual" has several different meanings!** Speaking of socks, I can't be blamed for the Steelers' defeat last weekend. I did wear my Steelers' socks on Sunday (game day). So it must have been someone else's feet that can be blamed for their loss in the final minute of the game.

There are certain Sundays which preachers dread.....this is one of them! This weekend commemorates a number of events and there are groups within the diocese and parish which expect me to say something about each of them in the sermon. To name a few:

1. This is the unofficial **Vocations Awareness Sunday**, so I should say something about the life and work of priests, deacons, and religious.

2. This is the 48th anniversary of the opening of the **Second Vatican Council**, so I should say something about the work in our Church begun by the Council.

3. This week marks the 32nd anniversary of the election of Pope John Paul II, so I should say something about Pope John Paul II who guided our church for so many years.

4. On Monday, we celebrate **Columbus Day** and the 518th anniversary of the discovery of America, so I should say something about that, and probably about the **Knights of Columbus** right here in our parish.

5. This is also our normal parish Sunday Mass, so the liturgical police tell me I should preach only about the assigned readings (which, by the way, speak notably about lepers!).

6. And for all our Canadian visitors and snowbirds, Monday is the **Canadian National Thanksgiving Day** so I should make some mention of that because we are very grateful for all the folks who visit us from Canada each week.

There is probably **NO WAY** any preacher can preach about all these things in one sermon, but I love a challenge so I'm going to do it!

IN EACH OF THE THINGS MENTIONED ABOVE, SOMEONE SAW A TRUTH AND ACTED UPON IT. Therein lies the connection!

1. NAAMAN the Syrian in today's First Reading saw the truth that the God of Israel could cure his leprosy, so he did something about it.....he went to Israel.

2. The **UNNAMED SAMARITAN LEPER** in today's Gospel saw the truth that Jesus had indeed healed him, so he did something about it....he went back to Jesus with his thanks.

3. **CHRISTOPHER COLUMBUS** recognized the truth that the world was round and much larger than many of his contemporaries ever imagined.....so he set sail across thousands of uncharted miles of ocean bringing, among other things, the Catholic Faith with him.

4. **PEOPLE WHO BECOME PRIESTS, DEACONS, OR RELIGIOUS** recognize the truth the God has called them to serve His Catholic Church in a special way so they act upon it.....they willingly serve the Lord and commit their lives to Him.

5. **THOSE WHO CHARTED THE COURSE OF VATICAN II** recognized the truth that the Catholic Church had to express itself in some new ways and so they acted as best they could on this truth.

6. **THOSE WHO SETTLED CANADA REALIZED THAT THEY HAD MUCH FOR WHICH TO BE THANKFUL** so they chose a day to annually renew their sense of gratitude.

7. **THE KNIGHTS OF COLUMBUS** here in our parish saw the truth that Catholic men need to band together to support each other, so they are part of a worldwide organization that provides them with many opportunities to be there for their brother knights and for the whole

community. They ran a hugely successful Yard Sale last month which netted a profit of over $3000.00 for their charitable works.

DID ALL THESE THINGS HAPPEN PERFECTLY? NO!

DID ALL THESE PEOPLE ACT WITH PURE AND TOTALLY SINCERE MOTIVATIONS ALL OF THE TIME? NO!

NAAMAN still belonged to a nation which oppressed God's people.
The **CURED SAMARITAN** might not have changed his views about the other Jewish people besides Jesus.

CHRISTOPHER COLUMBUS brought the Catholic Faith, but he also brought disease and colonialism to the new world.

PRIESTS, DEACONS, AND RELIGIOUS can sometimes be selfish and sinful.

VATICAN II's legacy of change hasn't always been helpful to the Church.

CANADA has the usual problems of nations in the Western Hemisphere ranging from unemployment to unrest.

OUR KNIGHTS OF COLUMBUS COUNCIL is still looking for some more Catholic men to join in their work.

The point is: **NONE OF US ARE PERFECT!** But all of us can have our moments of recognizing truth. And when we do recognize a truth, when we do see where God is leading us, then we too must be willing to act upon it. God has not called us because we **ARE** saints, but because with His help we can **BECOME** saints. **Even the Pope, I'm sure, has bad days!**

518 years ago on a small ship crossing a very large ocean, there was a prayer said each morning of the long and dangerous voyage. According to tradition, this prayer was lead not by the oldest or the wisest. It was lead by the youngest. Today, within this Mass, we offer this very same simple prayer in union with those who have gone before us in acting upon God's truth. And we ask God to help us to see, to appreciate and to act upon His truth in our own lives. Please repeat this prayer line by line after me:

Blessed by the Lord of day, and the holy cross.
Blessed be the Lord of truth, and the Holy Trinity.
Blessed be the immortal soul, and the Lord Who keeps it whole.
Blessed be the light of day, and the Lord Who sends the night away.

Amen.

There, I did it, 7 different topics covered in one sermon!
After the noon Mass, I think I'll go to the parish picnic,
eat and drink, and then take the rest of the day off!

God bless you!

29th Sunday in Ordinary Time - "C"

17 October 2010

FIRST READING: Exodus 17:8-13
PSALM: Psalm 121:1-8
SECOND READING: 2 Timothy 3:14 - 4:2
GOSPEL: Luke 18:1-8

"I felt like a new man when I woke up!"

What a great week for eating here in Paradise! About 60 people came to our parish picnic last Sunday at the church and they brought tons of great food (and I scarfed up some leftovers!). The lemon squares and baked beans were the absolute best! I wish I knew who had made them. Maybe next year we can put signs in front of each of the foods with the maker's name and phone number on them.

But the eating didn't stop there! I received a gift of fruit and nut mix from a snowbird from Michigan, and homemade sourdough bread, and homemade chicken and shrimp fajitas, and an incredible desert made from crumbled Snickers Bars, mixed with CoolWhip and cream cheese and diced apples. **It was like eating a caramel apple with a spoon!** And then there was the Laughlin Chefs' Food Fest on Thursday night which was described as a cornucopia of cuisine! And I prayed the invocation at the installation of our new Laughlin Postmaster on Friday...and someone made these incredible individual strawberry shortcakes! **Some people eat to live, sometimes I think I live to eat!**

And speaking of food, there is a contest being sponsored by Pop Tarts. To win, you have to describe what you would do with 1,000,000 Pop Tarts that would be a good advertisement for the company. Well, I've thought about it and thought about it, and I have come up with what I am sure will be the prize-winning entry in the contest! I can't tell you right now because I don't want someone else using my idea! But trust me, I feel sure I'm going to win! And the prize is awesome....I'll get 1,000,000 Pop Tarts!

I stopped at CVS to print some pictures. The girl at the checkout counter printed out my receipt and noticed that I had won a prize of a whole bag of Brach's Candy Corn. As she was handing it to me, she had to go and comment: **"Why do people of your generation like these things? We can't give them away at all to the young people!"** Welcome to my world!

A pastor once gave an unusually long sermon on prayer on the Sunday when the parable of the poor widow and the corrupt judge was read at church like today. Later, at the door, while the pastor was shaking hands with the departing congregation, one man said, **"Father, your sermon today was simply wonderful - so invigorating, so inspiring, and so refreshing."** The pastor, of course, broke out in a huge smile only to hear the man finish his statement of praise with, **"I felt like a new man when I woke up!"**

I'm not going to risk that comment on my fragile ego this weekend, so here's a brief story about prayer that you may enjoy.

Little Tom wanted a pocketknife, a Swiss Army knife, for his birthday. He told his mother, his dad, his grandma, and his grandpa, too. He told aunts and uncles and even his teacher at **pre-school** that he was going to get a pocket knife for his birthday. But when his birthday came, he didn't get the knife. How do you think he felt?

So Tom started thinking about Christmas. Christmas was a long way away, but he told everybody that he was going to get the pocket knife for Christmas. But the big day did arrive, and Tom eagerly opened every present. But there was no knife. Why do you think that Tom hadn't gotten a knife? But Tom never gave up the desire. When he got old enough to handle a pocket knife safely and show his parents that he was really responsible in taking care of things, he got his knife. His greatest wish came true.

When we pray to God, we pray for people and things, and sometimes it seems that God has heard our prayer right away. Other times, it seems that God does not even hear us. It seems that God has forgotten us. It seems that we are wasting our time even praying to God. But, like Tom's parents, God hears us. God answers every prayer. Sometimes though, like Tom's parents, God feels that we are not ready for the things we want. But God wants us to keep on praying as well as listening to Him speaking to us through His word in the Holy Scriptures, and never give up looking and asking for the very best things for ourselves and for other people.

I think that all three readings remind us of the same thing today: **NEVER GIVE UP!**

In **EXODUS**, Moses raised his hands in prayer, and as long as he prayed, the battle went in favor of the Israelites. His assistants, Aaron and Hur, supported him even when his hands grew tired. They never gave up seeking God's help.

In **PAUL'S LETTER TO TIMOTHY**, Paul reminds Timothy that he must **"REMAIN FAITHFUL, and CONTINUE TO PREACH WHETHER CONVENIENT OR INCONVENIENT, CONSTANTLY TEACHING AND NEVER LOSING PATIENCE."** Timothy is never supposed to give up doing what God asks of him.

In **LUKE'S GOSPEL** today, Jesus tells the story of the poor widow and the corrupt judge to remind His followers to **"PRAY ALWAYS AND NOT LOSE HEART"**. In other words, never give up!

Today's Scripture message comes through loud and clear: **NEVER GIVE UP!** Never give up on yourself, never give up on your family and neighbors and friends, never give up on your Catholic Faith, and never, never give up on God. We all need to be patient. **Remember little Tom and his pocketknife.**

God bless you!

Mac King and Charlie at MAGIC LIVE.

Lance Burton and Charlie at Magic Live!

30th Sunday in Ordinary Time - "C"

24 October 2010

FIRST READING: Sirach 35:12-14, 16-18
PSALM: Psalm 34:2-3, 17-19, 23
SECOND READING: 2 Timothy 4:6-8, 16-18
GOSPEL: Luke 18: 9-14

"There is nothing wrong with pointing out the flaws of people you care about as long as you are in their lives long enough to assist them in overcoming their flaws." (Michael Rene Serrano)

My brother Michael is back home after some months in NYC. We make a cool but odd pair. He's a 40 year old singer/actor, tall & muscular massage therapist/personal trainer. I guess we don't look much alike at all! (And the fact that his ancestry is Jamaican/Puerto Rican only adds to us not resembling each other!) **Because he thinks that I have a God-complex, he likes to try to keep me humble.** Sometimes he criticizes me for not listening well enough. After he critiques me about something, he'll add something like: **"I only beat you down so I can build you back up again!"** or **"There is nothing wrong with pointing out the flaws of people you care about as long** as you are in their lives long enough to assist them in overcoming their flaws."

One night we found a two-man script about a man talking with God, so we decided to act it out for fun and practice. Before we had even talked about which part to take, he said, **"You'll probably want the God part....I know how you think!"** And he was right! And then, after I got a cool new shirt with dollar signs on it, some friends started calling me **"Jackpot"** as a nickname! When Michael said it, I suggested that it be changed to **"Jackpot Charlie"**. And he immediately said, **"Yeah, right, so you can have the initials JC. I knew you wanted to be God!"**

Last week, we were watching a movie called **THE ANSWER MAN**. The premise of the story was that the leading character had written a best-selling book called **ME AND GOD** and it had achieved world-wide popularity. In the middle of the movie, Michael leaned over and said **"It's a good thing you didn't write that book."** When I asked him why he had said that, he replied, **"Because if you wrote it, it would be called ME AS GOD!"** He also thinks that sometimes my stories are boring, like last week when a group of us were talking and he asked a friend **"Can I borrow a couple of toothpicks so I can keep my eyes open until Charlie finishes his story!"**

Sometimes I think God put Michael into my life just to keep me humble.

Speaking of God, I love my memories as a high school teacher. One marking period, I assigned my freshman Latin class to write a brief paper about what they liked about the ancient Roman pagan religion. Our textbook had explained it as being a **"QUID PRO QUO"** religion and they asked me what **"QUID PRO QUO"** meant. I said it meant something like **"You do something for me, and I'll do something for you."** Some adults, I think, still use the phrase **"You scratch my back, I'll scratch yours."** When the papers came in, I was honestly amazed to discover that more than **HALF** of my freshmen **LIKED** that **"quid pro quo"** aspect of religion! They liked the idea that if they did certain things for God, then God was required to do an equal amount for them. I guess it made God manageable to them. But in thinking about it, I couldn't agree with them at all. When I consider the little I actually do for God in terms of time given over to him, money used for His Church, obedience freely given to His will, I am amazed at how much God gives to me! In fact, the more I think about it, the more I am **EXTREMELY GRATEFUL** that God **doesn't** give me an equal amount of what I give to Him! I mean just think about the people who run out of here before Mass is over....imagine if God treated them with an equal amount of His time and attention! That's downright scary.

The **PHARISEE** in today's Gospel had it all wrong too. Both he and the **TAX COLLECTOR** went to the Temple to pray. But the **PHARISEE** prayed by telling God how much he was doing for God, how much God needed him. The **TAX COLLECTOR**, on the other hand, prayed by asking God to do for him what he needed most in his life. The **TAX COLLECTOR** knew how much he needed God.

Sometimes, I think, we get it all wrong too. We pray and act as though God needed us, when in actual truth, we are the ones who need God so desperately in our lives. Just imagine what it would be like if God gave us the same exact amount of time and attention that we give to Him. Even a simple thing like leaving Mass early without any real reason seems to say that I don't want to give to God one more minute than I absolutely have to. Maybe this week would be a good time to take a few moments and just think a little about how very much each one of us needs God, and how very grateful we should be that God gives us so much more than we could ever give to Him.

I really do know that I'm not God.....even though Michael is still pretty sure that I sometimes still think that I am! But I really do know that I need God in my life, and you do too! When we pray, think of the PHARISEE and the TAX COLLECTOR. **Do we sometimes sound as though we need a reminder from Michael that there's only one God....and He's not you or me?**

God bless you!

Michael and Charlie on a casual night out!

31st Sunday in Ordinary Time - "C"

31 October 2010

FIRST READING: Wisdom 11:22 - 12:2
PSALM: Psalm 145:1-2, 8-11, 13-14
SECOND READING: 2 Thessalonians 1:11 - 2:2
GOSPEL: Luke 19:1-10

It is good for us to know our place in the universe.

Just so you know, this has been **National Magic Week!** Another amazing week! Michael and I drove out to LA to spend two days with Eddie and Andy. On the way, we had to stop at Baker to see the **World's Tallest Thermometer.** Not as exciting as I thought it might be, but still fun. Got to see the famous Hollywood sign and walked the beach in Santa Monica. Spent one night at the famous **Magic Castle** in Hollywood. Walking down the main street in Burbank with the kids, they asked if I would ever think of living in Burbank. I said **"maybe"** and they said there were some great **"SENIOR CITIZEN"** apartments for rent near them! We went to Barney's Beanery, a bar in Burbank, and were having a beer watching the LA Lakers' game. Every time the Lakers scored, the crowd in the bar would stand up and cheer. I commented to Michael, **"Gee, I wonder why there sure** are a lot of **Lakers' fans here."** And he just rolled his eyes, looked down at me condescendingly, and said, **"We're in LA!"** Sometimes I feel like Rodney Dangerfield.....I just get no respect!

And I've got a huge decision facing me this weekend....do I cheer for the **STEELERS** or for the **SAINTS** on Sunday? There are some people who think that I have to be on the side of the **SAINTS**, but I think I'm going for the **STEELERS**. After all, I intend to spend eternity with the saints, so they won't mind if I go with the Steelers this weekend!

While it's not my favorite holiday, I really do love Halloween even as I'm getting older. I remember one Halloween as an adult where I got dressed as a giant OWL. The kids at the parish school loved it so much that I decided to keep the costume on all day! I even went to the bank to make a deposit from the parish. You would be amazed to learn that people still get nervous when someone walks into a bank wearing a mask! And since I couldn't talk clearly through the mask, I handed the bank teller a note saying **"Happy Halloween!"** Needless to say, I was escorted out of the bank by police with guns! On another Halloween, I didn't have time for a costume, so I just headed over to a party dressed as a priest. Everyone asked me how I was able to get such a realistic-looking priest outfit!

Sometimes I am no good at guessing what costumes some of the children are wearing. One year, I was at a party for some pre-school kids. Among their costumes, there was a spaceman, a mermaid, a pumpkin, a cat, a NASCAR driver. I think I got into trouble though. One of the little kids was all dressed in pink fur. I had no idea what she was. So I said, **"Nice whatever you are!"** Her mother informed me that she was bunny rabbit, but had lost her bunny ears and nose! How was I supposed to know? And then there was the little girl dressed completely in black and white blotches. So I looked at her and said **"Nice cow!"** Her mother, a little perturbed, said **"She's a dalmation!"**

Halloween is the one time of the year when we all really admit that sometimes we try to be someone we're not, when we really admit to putting on masks to cover up our real selves. And today's readings from the Book of Wisdom and from the Gospel of St. Luke are good reminders for us of just who we really are. **IT IS GOOD FOR US TO KNOW OUR PLACE IN THE UNIVERSE.** While the whole universe can be described as a single grain of wheat or a drop of dew, God chooses to love us because He has made us and because He keeps us in existence. And just as Jesus in the Gospel seeks out the real Zacchaeus because He loves him, so Jesus continues to seek out our real selves.

If somebody, anybody, cares enough about me to try to find out what I'm really like deep down inside, it is impressive to me. And today's readings suggest that it is God Himself Who is trying to get behind my mask, to get through to the real me because He really loves and cares for me. And like †, if we are willing to let God behind our masks, I think we'll find that we don't need the masks so much anymore. We won't have to try to look happy, we'll really be happy. We won't have to try to appear holy, we'll really be holy. And we won't have to pretend to be interested in one another's well-being, because by allowing God within our hearts and selves, we'll feel the need to share God and God-like qualities with others. **Faith leads us to do things that faith-filled people do.**

I always get interesting Halloween cards, but the best one I ever received was several years ago and read: **"This year for Halloween I'm going to change you into a big, ugly toad....and while I'm at it, are there any other improvements you would like me to make?"** Except for the "big, ugly toad" part, I think God is offering us His power to make whatever improvements need to be made in each one of us. We don't need to hide our real selves, God already loves us because He created us and keeps us in existence. What we need to do is to see things as God sees them and willingly let God make whatever improvements need to be made in our lives.

By the way, I'd like to suggest that you keep that idea in your mind on Tuesday when you go to vote for local, state and national leaders. **Pray that you will see things as God sees them**, and not just the masks that politicians sometimes put on display before an election. **Your Catholic Faith got you here on Sunday; that same Catholic Faith should guide you in making the right decisions on Tuesday.**

God bless you!

Eddie and Andy and Charlie at Disneyland!

32nd Sunday in Ordinary Time - "C"

7 November 2010

FIRST READING: 2 Maccabees 7:1-2, 9-14
PSALM: Psalm 17:1, 5-6, 8, 15
SECOND READING: 2 Thessalonians 2:16 - 3:5
GOSPEL: Luke 20:27-38

"Everyone wants to go to heaven, but no one wants to go now!"

I had a lot of **FIRSTS** this week. My friend Bruce and I had lunch at **Le Cordon Bleu**, the culinary institute in Las Vegas. The food was spectacular, and artistically presented. The restaurant operation is part of the course for the students there. We began our meal with bowls of cream of butternut squash soup, with dollops of sour cream and fresh cracked pepper. The staff was very attentive. Before we began to eat, Bruce and I prayed as we always do. The waiter came right over and told us: **"You know, you two are the only guys I've ever seen pray in here!"** I guess you never know who's watching when you pray!

And I went to **CORNFEST** on Friday night over in Arizona. What a fun time! Lots of games and things to do! Saw some magic and balloon creations, won a few prizes by tossing rolls of toilet paper into a mock toilet (What a great game!), and had my first encounter with a chiropractor! There was this guy there who asked us if we had ever been to a chiropractor. We all said **"No"**. He was running a special. Give him $10 and he would **"adjust"** your body. Well, no one else was willing, but I figured $10 was a good investment, and I'd never had my body adjusted. So I lay down on this table and he starts pushing on my back....felt good...and then he grabbed me, pulled me over on my side, shoved my knee up into my stomach, and pulled me towards him! I could hear all sorts of crackling noises! After he did that a few times, he started messing with my neck, and told me not to be afraid. If it all started to go dark, and I felt like I was in a long tunnel, I should just go to the light! With that, he twisted my head to the right, and then to the left! There was a whole series of crackling sounds! All I can say is that when I stood up and realized that all my bones were still intact, it felt wonderful!

And I got a call this week from a guy I went to kindergarten with back in New Jersey. I hadn't seen Dennis in almost 40 years. He was visiting in Prescott, Arizona, and wanted to drive over to see me. It was kind of funny talking with him since we've had practically no contact in all that time. We reminisced about the old neighborhood and he told me about this really cool website called **VPIKE.com** where you could go and type in your address and it would show you a satellite picture of the house and street. The amazing thing is that you could actually walk down the street and see all the houses. It's not real time, but it is fairly recent. Kind of scary that from somewhere out in space, a camera could see so much of my life! It was a lot of fun checking out loads of places with the site. Kind of makes me feel that "Big Brother" could be watching....

But one of the things Dennis wanted to tell me was that even when he went through quintuple bypass surgery some years ago, he wasn't afraid of death....and he said that I was responsible for that. Man, that got my attention! He said that when his father died, I had done the funeral back in 1974 when I had just been ordained. And he remembered how I had said that death is so much a part of life, we're all going to do it. In fact, he said, he had figured out the leading cause of death. I asked him what the leading cause of death was....and he told me: **"Birth!"** At any rate, he wanted me to know that I was the first one to have taught him that and he was grateful.

The chiropractor and Dennis' visit were just some of the events recently that conspired to remind me that this might be an opportune weekend to speak about death. We celebrated All Saints Day on November 1st, and then All Souls Day on November 2nd. We got word that Father Peter Romeo, a former administrator here at St. John's had died on All Saints Day. All three of our readings for Mass this weekend speak of death and eternity. So I want to offer just a few simple thoughts on the topic for us to consider this week.

No day ever goes by that death does not come to some member of the human family. In time, all those we love take the final step in their journey to God, their Father and Creator. We lose parents, spouses, brothers, sisters, sons, daughters, relatives and dear friends. We treasure the love and joy they brought to our lives, and because we love them, we rightly feel the pain of being separated from them. Even the deaths of people not personally known to us - our soldiers in Iraq and Afghanistan, killed by evil terrorists - cause us to feel grief at their loss.

There are many ways of speaking about DEATH and LIFE-AFTER-DEATH, but we have to be careful not to get so entangled in the details that we lose sight of the reality. **We fear death because we fear the unknown.** All we can know for sure is life, and death, it seems to us, is the opposite of life and so we are fearful of it. I recall an old priest once saying in a funeral sermon: **"Everyone wants to go to heaven, but no one wants to go now!"** How true.

The **SADDUCEES** in today's Gospel seek a way to trap Jesus in details about death and life-after-death, but Jesus won't let Himself be trapped in the details. Whenever Jesus spoke of death, He spoke in terms of life, terms with which we are familiar. He said things like: **"I AM THE WAY AND THE TRUTH AND THE LIFE. WHOEVER LIVES AND BELIEVES IN ME WILL LIVE FOREVER. NO ONE COMES TO THE FATHER EXCEPT THROUGH ME. I AM GOING TO PREPARE A PLACE FOR YOU SO THAT WHERE I AM, THERE YOU ALSO MAY BE."** Every part of our life in Christ here on earth is a preparation for our life in Christ after death. When death comes to a person who has lived Christ's way of life on earth, it will not be the end of his/her life; it will be the first split second of a new and brighter life. We don't know the details of **HOW** this will happen; in fact, we don't need to know the details. We just need to know that God is always true to His word. **For those who believe, life is changed, not ended.** God said it, I believe it, that settles it.

Years ago, there was a wonderful series of books called **CHILDREN'S LETTERS TO GOD.** One such letter went like this: **"Dear God, what is it like when you die? Nobody will tell me. I just want to know. I don't want to do it! - Your friend, Mike."** I've often thought that a good answer might be: **"Dear Mike, what is it like** when you die? It's a lot like life, only much, much better! Just you wait and see! - Your friend, God."

As we remember our deceased loved ones in this month of November, may we pray for the faith to trust that God always keeps His word. May we always have the Faith to believe and to act accordingly. And maybe we should keep in mind a short and simple thought when things get fuzzy in our minds: **God said it, I believe it, that settles it!**

God bless you!

When Andrew Norelli comes to town!

33rd Sunday in Ordinary Time - "C"

14 November 2010

FIRST READING: Malachi 3:19-20
PSALM: Psalm 98:5-9
SECOND READING: 2 Thessalonians 3:7-12
GOSPEL: Luke 21:5-19

Nothing that happens happens outside the knowledge of God.

Another truly amazing week in Paradise! It was non-stop energy! I was thinking of a game I've played called **"I'll bet you didn't know"** in which each person has to go around and tell one thing about himself that the others in the group didn't know. It really is amazing! For example, I'll bet you didn't know that if I hadn't become a priest, I would have liked to have become a magician who does stand-up comedy in Vegas! And I'll bet you didn't know that my favorite movies are **HAROLD AND MAUDE** and **THE PUNISHER.**

HAROLD AND MAUDE is a cult classic about an 80 year old woman who's in love with life and who sees only the good and beautiful in it, and a 17 year old boy who is fascinated with darkness and death and who sees only the dark side of things. They become friends by meeting at funerals...she goes because she loves the flowers, he goes because he's fascinated by death.

THE PUNISHER is based on the comic book of the same name and while it sounds scary, it really is a comedy because of its comic book style. My favorite scene is the torture scene where the hero (THE PUNISHER played by Thomas Jane) has the victim hanging upside down in a warehouse and he carefully heats up a metal rod until it is white hot. He shows it to the victim and explains that he's going to plunge it into him from the back and that it is **"so hot, it will feel ice cold as it goes in."** The victim, of course, is terrified and screaming. In fact, all the Punisher does is walk behind the victim and take out a frozen popsicle and gently run it down the victim's back! And then he just walks away while the victim thinks he's been fatally burned.

And I'll bet some of our visitors didn't know that one of my favorite Vegas shows is Frank Marino's Divas Las Vegas! So you can imagine how much I enjoy it when the show is in Laughlin for this week. Now I admit that some of my friends think it is a little weird for me to enjoy a female impersonators' show so much, but it truly is a really amazing show! And over the years out here, I'm blessed to call several members of the cast my friends. So if you saw me being hugged by Joan Rivers, or Dolly Parton, or a tall guy with a Mohawk, or this ripped guy

(Paul) who is the dance captain, it's okay....they're just friends. Some of us went out bowling after the show one night this week, and I'm proud to say I actually bowled better than one of them! Yeah, all the others beat me embarrassingly! And we did go to one of the Riverside bars one night, and the bartender carded us for age! Well, I kind of held back, but then he said **"You too, Mister!"** I knew it was pity, but I pulled out my driver's license anyway! He then asked what parts we all did in the show, and Paul piped up right away that he was looking at Madonna, Cher, and then pointed at me and said **"He's Tina Turner!"** There's a funny monologue at the beginning of the show. Has a little strong language in it, but nothing most folks haven't heard on TV. And seeing Cher, Whitney Houston, Dolly Parton, Joan Rivers, Tina Turner, Celine Dion, Beyonce and so many others come alive is great entertainment. I took Eddie to see the show, and he fell in love with Britney Spears. I had to keep poking him and telling him: **"Eddie, it's a guy!"** If you go, tell them Father Charlie sent you. It will make some great guys smile.

Okay, I admit it's weird, but it is funny in a weird sort of way.

And speaking of weird.....do you remember the scary things we were reading about 10 years ago as we approached the dawning of the new millennium with the coming of the new year 2000? People were predicting the end of the world, the crash of the stock market, asteroids destroying the earth, tidal waves engulfing continents, a computer meltdown, and so many more terrible calamities. The coming of the year 2000 really scared some people in thinking about the end of the world. And if you follow current events on the Internet, you know that another round of scare tactics is brewing because some people think the world will end on December 21, 2012. Lots of graphic stuff being written about that. But I think I'll be sending out Christmas cards that year anyway!

Well, today's readings speak rather graphically about the end of the world as they do every year at this time. And it certainly is hard to just gloss over them, especially when they contain phrases like:

THE DAY IS COMING...BLAZING LIKE AN OVEN.....IT WILL ALL BE TORN DOWN, NOT ONE STONE WILL BE LEFT ON ANOTHER.....NATION WILL RISE AGAINST NATION, KINGDOM AGAINST KINGDOM, GREAT EARTHQUAKES, PLAGUES, FAMINES IN VARIOUS PLACES....AND IN THE SKY FEARFUL OMENS AND GREAT SIGNS.

But as scary as these words might be about the end of the world, I don't think the end of the world scares us nearly as much as the fears we have to face each day of our lives. Even as we gather for Mass this weekend, there are people among our parishioners, and families and friends who are worried about:

finding a job

graduating from college

facing the loneliness of living alone now that a wife or husband has died

growing old and fearing the loss of one's health

dealing with the sickness or death of a child

dealing with a parent with cancer or alzheimer's or both

worrying about friends with HIV/AIDS

worrying about paying this month's bills

And the list goes on and on. **Most of us are not nearly as worried about the end of the world as we are about making it to the end of the day.**

I can't take any of these worries away, no one can. They are real parts of our lives. But our Faith can offer some hope to those who try to be faithful. After all, that's one of the reasons why we gather each Sunday to hear and strengthen our faith and hope. And the words of hope are these:

Nothing that happens happens outside the knowledge of God. He is aware of what we go through and He is concerned about it. His love is constant no matter what. That doesn't mean that we won't have problems

or worries, but it does mean that we never have to face the future alone. God's love is constant, there is nothing that we ever have to face alone without God. NOTHING. Neither the end of the world, nor the end of the day.

So, whatever your worries are, whatever you are facing in life today, just try to place your hand securely in God's hand. He knows and He cares. It's not easy to maintain faith, but sometimes it is all we have. Hold on to it.

God bless you!

The Solemnity of Our Lord Jesus Christ the King

21 November 2010

FIRST READING: 2 Samuel 5:1-3
PSALM: Psalm 122:1-5
SECOND READING: Colossians 1:12-20
GOSPEL: Luke 23:35-43

"TAPAS, Eddie, TAPAS. Do you honestly think I would ever take you to a topless bar?"

What an awesome week! Lots of great food! Lots of fun up in Vegas as we celebrated Eddie's 27th birthday. Michael, Andy and I took him out to Firefly, a tapas bar in Las Vegas, just like we did last year. I love tapas....small plates of great foods that we all could share as we sipped sangria by a fireplace in the evening. Of course, I had to remember that last year, when we first took Eddie to the tapas bar, he got all confused and was looking around like something was missing. When we asked him what he was looking for, he said: **"You guys promised to take me to a topless bar!"**...."**TAPAS, Eddie, TAPAS. Do you honestly think I would ever take you to a topless bar?"** Ah, good times, good times....

There's a wonderful old saying that **"One picture is worth a thousand words."** Today, as we celebrate the **FEAST OF CHRIST THE KING**, I would like to put that old saying into practice. I invite you to sit back, watch and listen as our picture develops.

1. **CHAIR** - This chair is like a throne. Each one of us has a throne, a seat of power, in our lives. Whoever or whatever sits upon this throne governs the way the other persons and things in our lives function.

2. These are some of the other persons and things in our lives:

A. **Stuffed animal (toys, luxuries, possessions) KOALA**

B. Food/Drink - ORIGINAL SIN - RICE SNACKS

C. Money - DOLLAR BILLS - MONEY TRAY

D. Power - position - CLERGY SHIRT – BIRETTA

E. Looks - MIRROR – SUNGLASSES

F. Family/Friends - RIO PICTURE of MOM - THE FAMILY

G. Work - BRIEFCASE PACK

H. God - CROSS

I. Sin - HANDCUFFS

3. All of these, except for **SIN**, are good. All of these, **including SIN**, try to occupy the throne of our lives. No matter which one gets on the throne, the other persons and things have to find a place around the throne and compete for a position.

But there is only one Person who has the **right** to that throne – **CHRIST THE KING**. If Christ is seated on the throne of our lives, then all the other persons and things will eventually find their rightful place.

It's that simple....either Christ is in charge or everything else is out of whack.

LORD, YOU ARE OUR KING AND WE ARE YOUR FAITHFUL AND GRATEFUL PEOPLE.

WHEN WE PRAY IN THE OUR FATHER "THY KINGDOM COME", HELP US TO REALIZE THAT YOUR KINGDOM IS ALREADY AT WORK IN OUR HEARTS AND IN OUR LIVES.

MAY WE WORK WITH ALL THAT WE HAVE AND

ALL THAT WE ARE TO MAKE YOUR KINGDOM A REALITY IN THIS WORLD.

THY KINGDOM COME.

MAY IT COME SOON.

God bless you!

The First Sunday of Advent - "A"

28 November 2010

FIRST READING: Isaiah 2:1-5
PSALM: Psalm 122:1-9
SECOND READING: Romans 13:11-14
GOSPEL: Matthew 24:37-44

So, we must not let Christmas be taken away from us.

Thanksgiving Dinner was awesome! Michael came down from Las Vegas, Eddie and Andy came in from Los Angeles. So my whole family was together for dinner. For the benefit of the visitors, Michael is my brother. He's Puerto Rican/Jamaican so we don't look much alike! Eddie is my "illegitimate son" (the locals can explain this to you!), and Andy has been adopted as the "weird nephew" in our family! None of us have families out here in the West, so we decided that we're making our own family. They decided that we would all be together for Thanksgiving dinner here in Laughlin, and Michael would cook. I was a little worried. I have never used the stove in the rectory. I have a microwave, what do I need a stove for? And Michael never lets me near him when he's cooking. But we are making progress. He let me do something this year. He sent me out to get ranch dip. And then he sent me out to get foil. And then he sent me out to get storage bags. When I asked if there was something I could do in the kitchen and not in my car, he handed me 10 cranberries and told me to find a knife and cut them into very small pieces. I think he was just trying to get rid of me. But it was the best Thanksgiving dinner ever! Lots of laughing, talking, joking, and, of course, eating!

We did have a little excitement. On the way to Laughlin from LA, Eddie and Andy blew out two tires on Route 40 just outside of Needles while drive over 70 mph. I drove down to get them and we arranged for the car to be towed. Eddie wasn't wearing a seatbelt and could have been ejected from the car when it ran off the road and nearly flipped. When I saw he was okay, I grabbed him around the neck and told him that if he had been killed because of not wearing a seatbelt, I would have killed him. He later explained the lack of logic in what I said, but appreciated the sentiment! And he promised to wear his seatbelt from now on.

Now that Thanksgiving is over, the countdown to Christmas has begun! Just 27 more days, and Christmas will be here...and there is so much to do! So let me get on my soapbox and begin!

For some reason, that generically bland, but oh so politically correct greeting, **"Happy Holidays"** that has all but drowned out the much older and much more correct **"Merry Christmas"** in American society is bothering me more and more. As Catholic Christians, we are **not** preparing to celebrate the winter solstice or the winter holidays or any other generically-named festival. We are preparing to celebrate the annual remembrance of one particular historical event on December 25th - the birth of Jesus Christ, the Savior of the World, in Bethlehem some 2000 years ago.

Loudly and clearly we need to proclaim our faith in Jesus Christ, and all that Christmas celebrates about God Himself becoming a part of the human race and living on this planet for some 33 years before giving His life on the cross for the salvation of the world. As important as Easter is, Christmas is vitally important in the history of salvation too. **In fact, if there were no Christmas, there would be no Easter either.**

So, we must not let Christmas be taken away from us. As nice as trees and snowmen and lights and reindeer and Santa might be, the true symbol of Christmas is the Nativity Scene - the manger with Jesus, Mary and Joseph, the sheep and cattle, the shepherds, the wise men, camels, the angels, and the shining star.

Now I know that there are some people whose family tradition is to hold back placing the Baby Jesus in the manger until Christmas, but without the Baby Jesus, it's just a bunch of people and camels and sheep milling around! I really think that we need to do what we can to make sure that no one doubts our Faith in the true meaning of Christmas. So perhaps setting up your Nativity set early might help keep a few more people focused on **WHO** we're really getting ready for on December 25th.

And before someone reports me to the liturgical police, yes I did authorize our music people to have us sing **"SILENT NIGHT"** at every Sunday Mass between now and Christmas....just to keep us focused on what Christmas really is about. Speaking of the liturgical police, there are some people in the church who are really extreme about what can or cannot be done, said, sung in the liturgy. In the seminary, we had a joke. **Do you know the difference between a LITURGIST and a TERRORIST?** The answer is: **You can negotiate with a terrorist!** And speaking of liturgists, next year, in Advent, we will all be adjusting to the new translations for the Mass that will be put into effect. We'll be doing a lot of preparation for that during 2011. Some of the translations are a little awkward or stilted in their terminology and I had to laugh when I read one liturgist who wrote: **"It's more important to be correct than to**

be understandable." But that's a topic for another sermon.

And certainly the world situation prompts us to focus our thoughts on the peace that only Jesus Christ can bring. We need to pray fervently and frequently that the message of peace and hope that Jesus brought into the world on that first Christmas day will somehow overcome the violence and unrest in our world community. Isaiah's image of God's holy mountain in today's first reading where nations come to live in peace is surely not yet a reality. So we should also be reminded to pray for those in our military forces who will not be able to spend Christmas with their families. We owe so much to those brave men and women, particularly those spending Christmas in the dangers of Iraq and Afghanistan, and places throughout the world.

Jesus is the Reason for the season. Christmas without Jesus is just unthinkable. As we go through these Advent weeks of preparation, let's keep alert and awake and know that without Jesus there would be no Christmas for anyone. Advent begins today - let's start getting our homes and hearts and minds and souls ready for Christmas. It will be here sooner than we can imagine. The countdown has begun!

God bless you!

Eddie , Charlie, Jason and Andy just hanging out one day!

The Second Sunday of Advent - "A"

5 December 2010

FIRST READING: Isaiah 11:1-10
PSALM: Psalm 72:1-2, 7-8, 12-13, 17
SECOND READING: Romans 15:4-9
GOSPEL: Matthew 3:1-12

"He's now in the biggest production show of his career - heaven."

Another amazing week in Paradise! Here it is the first week of December, and I'm still wearing a short-sleeved shirt! **New Jersey was never like this!** If I didn't live here already, I'd be a coming here as a snowbird for sure! Had several surprises this past week. On a sad note, my friend David Reynolds was killed in a head-on car crash the night before Thanksgiving out near Palm Springs. He was only 45. I drove out to Palm Springs to do his Memorial Service on Tuesday. For all of us, it was a reminder of just how quickly our lives can change. David and I go back more than 10 years. He was an extremely talented singer/dancer/actor. As one of his friends told me - **"He's now in the biggest production show of his career - heaven."** I liked that thought. It's kind of the theatrical version of **"He's in a better place."** So true.

And I got surprise guests on Thursday night just before midnight. Eddie and Andy drove in from Los Angeles. I think they were worried about how I was doing because of my friend's death, but they would never admit that! Fortunately, I don't need much sleep because we were up until 3:00 AM on Friday morning! They were discussing the idea of just making it an all-nighter, but I told them I needed some sleep! Made me feel really good when they actually got themselves out of bed for the 8AM Mass on Friday morning with me. It saved me having to wake them up. **In the past, I have found that beating Eddie's feet with a book or ring usually works pretty well.**

And I finally started my Christmas shopping since there are only a couple of weeks to go before Christmas. I like to find unusual things for my family and friends. Well, this year a lot of them have been talking about how much they all love bacon. So I actually found a website which sold **BACON-SCENTED** air fresheners, and **BACON-FLAVORED** drink tablets! Ah, when I think of the joy on their faces when they open their presents, it just warms my heart!

Kind of makes you glad that you're not on my Christmas gift list!

There's a wonderful story of a man praying to God, and it goes like this:

"God" says the man.

"Yes" says God.

"Can I ask You a question?"

"Go right ahead."

"God, what is a million years to You?"

"A million years to Me is only a second."

"Hmmmmm.....God, what is a million dollars to You?"

"A million dollars to Me is like a penny"

"God, can I have a penny?"

"Sure," said God, "...just a second."

Life doesn't always happen at the speed with which we want it to happen. Things sometimes take more time and effort than we anticipated. And sometimes it is easy to get discouraged when things don't happen the way we want them to happen or as fast as we want them to happen. It's good for us to remember that God's timing is different than our own. And that things will happen in God's time, without delay.

The people of Israel waited for centuries for the coming of the Savior, and in God's own good time, Jesus came, was born, and lived among them. St. John the Baptist in today's Gospel comes to prepare the way for the Lord. He called people to get ready for the coming of the Savior. He knew that Jesus was coming and he wanted the people to be ready.

You and I are in a similar situation as we approach Christmas. We know Jesus is coming and we need to get things ready. Oh, it might take more time and effort than we had planned, but it is certainly worth every bit of time and effort we can put into it, because it will surely happen whether we're ready or not. And unexpected things might happen along the way.

So besides writing cards, buying and wrapping gifts, putting up beautiful decorations, preparing cookies, we also need to get our hearts and minds and souls ready for Christmas. For those who have been faithful, we just need to keep on being faithful and watchful. For those who have been lazy, we need to get ourselves back to the practice of our Catholic Faith while there is still time. Showing up on Christmas unprepared is not very smart. The Savior of the World is coming, and we need to get ready....while there is still time.

God bless you!

Charles and Father Charlie! The 8:00 AM Mass will never be the same!

The Third Sunday of Advent - "A"

12 December 2010

FIRST READING: Isaiah 35:3-6, 10
PSALM: Psalm 146:6-10
SECOND READING: James 5:7-10
GOSPEL: Matthew 11:2-11

"Charlie, they want models....not someone like you!"

Another amazing week in Paradise! And it included a homemade Lithuanian Kugel (Potato pie), some homemade caramel candy, a cheesecake, and a great parish Christmas Party for over 325 people on Friday night. If you were there, you got to see the magic of John Rotellini. John and I are off to Vegas on Sunday afternoon for a 3 show marathon on Sunday night. I suspect that Monday would not be a good day to ask me anything too complex until I get some sleep!

I was asked to write a Christmas article for our local paper, so I decided to write it about my favorite Christmas song. I was talking it over with Michael during the week and I commented that I'm sure many people would think that my favorite Christmas song would be **"Silent Night."** Without missing a beat, Michael commented **"No one who knows you would ever think anything about SILENT would be connected with you!"** I guess I do tend to talk a lot...... You'll have to read next week's local paper to find out what my favorite Christmas song really is.

Michael got a chance at a gig last week with Bobby Flay from the food network. They were going to be filming in Vegas and needed some models to be there in the background for one of Bobby Flay's presentations. I asked Michael if he had put in a good word for me to be in the show with him. He just looked at me and said, **"Charlie, they want models....not someone like you."** And that was my week.

Let me tell you about my friend Ken. Ken did 10 years in the Kansas State prison system before being released 4 years ago. He's done well for himself on the outside and got a degree as a welding inspector. He was living in Arkansas and he decided to come out to visit me at my parish in New Jersey, and on the Sunday he was there, we went out for breakfast with a few members of our choir. Ken and I talked about what we would say when someone finally asked **"Hey, how do you two know each other?"**

We, of course, decided to tell the truth, but to have some fun doing it. So when the question came up, I asked the choir members, **"What do you think?"** One suggested that Ken was a magician, another that he was a priest, another that he was someone from the military. Finally, we told them that Ken was doing time in a state prison and I started writing to him. It got real quiet. Then one choir member said to him, **"Did you kill anyone?"** and Ken said "No". Then another choir member said **"Did you cheat on your wife?"** and Ken said "No". After that we were fine. Apparently as long as Ken wasn't a killer or an adulterer, he was fine!

Like our choir, people often ask questions when they meet a new situation or new person. John the Baptist in today's Gospel sends his disciples to Jesus with a question, **"Are you the one who is to come, or should we look for another?"** Scripture scholars over the centuries have wondered why John did this. There are two possible explanations: (1) John really knew that Jesus was the Savior and he wanted his disciples to meet Jesus so that they would see that for themselves and follow Jesus. Or (2) John began to doubt that Jesus was the Savior because Jesus didn't conform to the popular Jewish beliefs that the Messiah (Savior) would be a warrior who would bring political, social and economic deliverance to Israel. John needed reassurance.

It's good for us to know that even John the Baptist needed reassurance. Maybe we should remember that if we sometimes have trouble believing. And John must have found it hard to realize that his work would be unfinished in his lifetime, that he was only getting things ready for Someone Else. But he came to recognize that Jesus was indeed the Savior, and so he directed his disciples to follow Jesus. He got them ready.

John the Baptist tried to get the world ready for Jesus. You and I have a little more than one week to try to get our hearts and homes and families and lives ready for Jesus. Oh, we may not finish everything, but let it be truly said of each one of us - we tried. Because at the end of our lives, God is not going to ask us if we have succeeded. God is only going to ask us if we tried.

So write those cards, buy those gifts, cook those meals, call those friends, wrap those packages....but try to remember that we're doing all this for the Lord. We're trying to get the world, our little part of it anyway, ready for the Lord to enter our hearts and the hearts of those around us. And all God asks of us at Christmas is that we try. In fact, that's all He ever asks of us throughout the year.

God bless you!

Jeffrey and Charlie in Vegas!

The Fourth Sunday of Advent - "A"

19 December 2010

FIRST READING: Isaiah 7:10-14
PSALM: Psalm 24:1-6
SECOND READING: Romans 1:1-7
GOSPEL: Matthew 1:18-24

"And you never miss the magic. It's always amazing to you."

Ah, I know that Christmas is coming! I've even received two fruitcakes already! And I got a call from a 78 year old lady in New Jersey who has known me for years. She called to assure me that she's running a little late, but that her homemade fruitcake will make it here to me in time for Christmas. Ah, life is good out here....really good!

I like to think that I do a pretty good job as a priest, but I have actually been told that I do my best in another job. **You know I love magic, but DOING magic isn't what I do best.** In fact, I haven't been able to learn a decent trick at all...but I'm still trying. I even have my Lance Burton 100 Magic Trick kit! I've known Lance since before he was really famous in Las Vegas and on TV. He's even remarked publicly that I've seen his show more often than anyone who doesn't actually work for the show. But his best comment was: **"Charlie, you make the best audience member for a magic show. You don't come to figure out the tricks; you come to be amazed. That's precisely the audience a magician is looking for. And you never miss the magic. It's always amazing to you."**

I was thinking of that as I saw Lance's Christmas card this week. And it occurred to me that the same concept might be true in other areas of our lives. For instance, why do we come to church every Sunday? Do we come to critique the sermon or see if the music fits our tastes? Do we come because our family makes us come? Do we come because we want people to think we are holy? Or rather, do we come because we know that God is here and God is going to amaze us with His generosity to us? If the sermon bores us, or the music isn't what we think it should be, or the person sitting next to us smells like mothballs or wet dog fur, so what? God is still here and God is still offering us more than we could possibly deserve. On the other hand, if the music is uplifting and the sermon thrills our souls, and the person sitting next to us smells like a forest in spring, well, that is just icing on the cake. It makes something already wonderful even more wonderful. The attitude with which we come to Mass on Sunday certainly affects us. Why, we could even miss the magic.

And what about Christmas coming in only a few more days....could we miss the magic of Christmas because of our attitudes? We could waste so much energy trying to figure out how the Virgin birth came about or what the Angel Gabriel looked like, or what year this all happened in, or why Joseph should believe in his dreams, etc. We could so analyze Christmas that we end up missing the sheer magic of it. God loves us so much that He choose to become one of us, part of creation itself.

If I were God, I might consider creating a world, adding a few oceans and some high snow-capped mountains. I'd probably even place it in a universe with a nice bright sun and moon and some really bright stars. I'd probably add plants and animals and even some people too. I can see myself creating and really enjoying it. **BUT THERE IS NO WAY I WOULD EVEN THINK ABOUT JOINING CREATION, BECOMING A PART OF IT!**

Christmas celebrates the fact that God loved us so much that He truly became one of us. If God Who can do anything He wants freely chooses to become part of the human race, isn't this truly amazing? If God has already done this for us, just imagine what He might be planning to do in the future!

Of all the greetings we receive at Christmas, the best one is still the one that Gabriel originally gave to Mary - think of it - **THE LORD IS WITH YOU**. And Christmas celebrates that **THE LORD IS WITH US TOO**. That is certainly amazing and certainly worth celebrating. Don't let anything going on in the world or even in your own lives keep you from missing the magic on Christmas. You're not coming to try to figure it out; you're coming to be amazed at the love God has for you. **Whatever you do this week, don't miss the magic of Christmas!**

God bless you!

Christmas Day - Mass at Midnight

25 December 2010

FIRST READING: Isaiah 9:1-6
PSALM: Psalm 96:1-3, 11-13
SECOND READING: Titus 2:11-14
GOSPEL: Luke 2:1-14

TODAY IS CHRISTMAS!

Well, it be politically correct, let me wish you a **HAPPY, MERRY, CHRISTMAHANUKAWANZA!** I think it's kind of interesting that so many stories in the USA have been promising delivery of gifts by December 25th, but trying O SO HARD to not admit that that date is significant. At least for today, let's scrap that politically-correct **JUNK** and admit what we all know to be true: **TODAY IS CHRISTMAS**....it's not the winter solstice or "the holidays". It's a **CHRISTMAS TREE**, not a Holiday Tree; and those are **CHRISTMAS CAROLS** that we're hearing on the radio, not just some holiday songs. We gather to celebrate the most significant event in human history since the creation of the world....God Himself was born in Bethlehem to live among us because He loves us!

A few days before Christmas, two young brothers were spending the night at their grandparents' house. When it

186

was time to go to bed, and anxious to do the right thing, they both knelt down to say their prayers. Suddenly, the younger one began to pray in a very loud shouting voice: **"Dear Lord, please ask Santa Claus to bring me a play-station, a mountain bike, and a telescope."** His older brother leaned over and nudged him and said: **"Why are you shouting? God isn't deaf!"** And the younger brother replied, **"I know, but Grandma is!"**

I love Christmas! It is a beautiful and magical time of the year. I love the Christmas greetings and cards from friends. And I love the cookies and other foods, especially the fruitcakes! **Did you know that there is a theory that there really is only ONE FRUITCAKE, but it gets passed around from family to family each year!** But suppose there was no Christmas, suppose Jesus Christ had never been born in Bethlehem. What would our lives be like?

No Christmas trees.....No Christmas decorations.....No Christmas lights.....No Santa Claus.....No Christmas presents.....No shopping for gifts.....No Christmas cards.....No Christmas vacation from school.....No "Silent Night", or "White Christmas" or "Rudolf the Red-Nosed Reindeer".....No one would be named Christopher, or Christian, or Christine.....December 25th would be an ordinary workday.....the year would be 2748 R.E. (Roman

Empire).....No Holy Week.....No Easter.....No Savior.....No Notre Dame Football.....No Christian universities, hospitals, high schools, grade schools, soup kitchens.....No churches, no priests, no sacraments. The world would be a very different place.

But Christ has come, and Christmas celebrates His coming. And we have so much for which to be thankful on Christmas.

If you woke up this morning with more health than illness, you are more blessed than the million people who won't survive this week.

If you have never experienced the danger of battle, the loneliness of imprisonment, the agony of torture or the pangs of starvation, you are ahead of 20 million people around the world.

If you can attend Mass each week without fear of harrassment, arrest, torture or death, you are more blessed than almost 3 billion people in the world.

If you have food in your refrigerator, clothes on your back, a roof over your head, and a place to sleep, you are richer than 75% of the world.

188

If you have money in the bank, money in your wallet, and spare change in a dish somewhere in your house, you are among the top 8% of the world's wealthiest.

If your parents are still married and still alive, you are very rare, and very fortunate.

If you can hold up your head with a smile on your face and are truly thankful, you are truly blessed because the majority can, but most do not.

If you can hold someone's hand, hug someone tightly, or even gently touch them on the shoulder, you are blessed because you can offer God's healing touch.

If you can read the Bible, or read the words of the songs we sing, you are more blessed than over 2 billion people in the world who cannot read anything at all.

If you have friends who love you and share their time with you, and share the all-year-long gift of real friendship with you, you are blessed beyond belief.

You are so blessed in ways you may never even know. And Christmas is a great time to remember your blessings and give thanks to God for them.

If Christ had not come, we'd be really in a bad way. But thanks be to God. Christ has come. And that's what Christmas is all about.

And speaking of friends.....

With all the so-called Politically-Correct approaches to this season, I received an email this week from my friend Ken, with the following greeting:

FOR OUR POLITICALLY-CORRECT FRIENDS:

Please accept with no obligation, implied or implicit, our best wishes for an environmentally conscious, socially responsible, low-stress, non-addictive, gender-neutral celebration of the winter solstice holiday, practiced within the most enjoyable traditions of the religious persuasion of your choice, or secular practices of your choice, with respect for the religious/secular persuasion and/or traditions of others or their choice not to practice religious or secular traditions at all. We also wish you a fiscally successful, personally fulfilling, and medically uncomplicated recognition of the onset of the generally accepted calendar year 2011, but not without due respect for the calendars of choice of other cultures whose contributions to society have helped make America great. Not to imply that America is necessarily greater than any other country. And without regard to the race, creed, color, age, physical ability, religious faith or sexual preference of the wishee or the wisher.

FOR ALL OUR NON-POLITICALLY-CORRECT FRIENDS:

Merry Christmas and a Happy New Year!

Christmas may not be politically correct, but it is historically significant and eternally worthwhile. Because of Christmas, things in this world are different and better. And there is an eternal gift of **HOPE** for all of us.

So from all of us here at St. John the Baptist, to all of you, Merry Christmas, and a Happy New Year!

God bless you!

The Holy Family of Jesus, Mary and Joseph

26 December 2010

FIRST READING: Sirach 3:2-6, 12-14
PSALM: Psalm 128:1-5
SECOND READING: Colossians 3:12-21
GOSPEL: Matthew 2:13-15, 19-23

Now, there's a fascinating thought....Jesus must have had friends when He was growing up.

I sure do hope that everyone had an amazing Christmas! I know I did! After 6 Christmas Masses, I drove up to be with my family in Vegas. Andy had gone home to spend Christmas with his parents in Minnesota. So that left just Michael, Eddie and me. I brought home a ton of cookies and cakes that had been given to me. Eddie went to the Dollar Store and bought half-price Santa hats. Michael deep-fried a turkey breast and then baked it until it fell apart with a fork and served it over pasta. We put on the Santa hats, finished off a lot of the cookies and lemon squares before dinner, and then ate turkey and pasta. We laughed and joked all afternoon, sprayed each other with water while doing the dishes, and reminisced about how 4 guys (Michael, Eddie, Andy and me) from 4 states (New Jersey, Wisconsin, Minnesota and Florida) and ranging in age from their 20's through their 60's should have all moved to Nevada and formed one weird but awesome family! **It was an amazing day!**

The Christmas holidays always bring a certain amount of nostalgia. Like many other folks I know, I call up or visit old friends. I even pull out some of the old photo albums. Maybe it's just the joy of seeing myself with lots of dark brown hair, or maybe it's the wonderful memories of the past. Whatever it is, it is good to be reminded of the old ties of family and friends, of the times spent together, of the lessons learned. Oh we all have relatives and friends that are a little **"unique"**, but that's what makes life so interesting. It drives some of my relatives crazy that I have one sign up in my room that reads: **"God gave us our relatives...thank God we can choose our friends."** And another sign that reads:

"Friends are God's apology for giving us families!" Those are two bits of wisdom that I learned from my Mom!

There aren't any photographs of Jesus and Mary and Joseph at home in Nazareth, or at any other time in Jesus' life. Imagine what the home movies and old photos of Jesus' family would have shown us. Jesus as a child sitting with Mary, or working in the family carpenter shop with Joseph, or playing outside with His friends. **(Now,** there's a fascinating thought....Jesus **must have had friends when He was growing up.)** Or think of the pictures that would have shown Jesus and His family visiting the Temple in Jerusalem or growing up in Nazareth. Thirty years went by in Nazareth, and Jesus grew into the Man whose life and teachings would change the whole world.

SOMETHING HAPPENED AT NAZARETH, something happened in Jesus' home and surroundings. When Jesus left Nazareth to begin His mission as Savior of the world, He was a Man of incredible power - the power to heal, to console, to forgive, to save.

SOMETHING HAPPENED AT NAZARETH that helped Jesus become the Man for others that Matthew, Mark, Luke and John would later write about in their Gospels; the Man that made Paul see us as chosen members of the Lord's own family who should imitate His own forgiveness and patience and kindness towards others. We may not have pictures of what happened at Nazareth, but we sure do have some very strong testimony that whatever happened there during those thirty formative years helped to make Jesus into a Man who would one day lay down His own life for the salvation of the world.

I wonder how many times in the course of His life Jesus must have thought back to those years in Nazareth, those people He knew and loved. I like to think that Jesus drew a lot of strength from those relationships with Mary and Joseph and His extended family and friends.

As we honor the Holy Family today, as we think about those thirty years at Nazareth, we might want to also think about our own families, our own friends, our own home towns now. Are we clothed with mercy and kindness? Can we forgive and bear with one another? Are we peaceful and thankful? Are these the memories that our families and friends will carry into life in the years ahead?

SOMETHING HAPPENED AT NAZARETH, something wonderful. Something is happening in our homes too. May it be something wonderful too.

God bless you!

Mary, the Mother of God

1 January 2011

FIRST READING: Numbers 6:22-27
PSALM: Psalm 67:2-3, 5-6, 8
SECOND READING: Galatians 4:4-7
GOSPEL: Luke 2:16-21

God bless you in 2011 and always!

Well, it was the coldest New Year's Eve on record for Las Vegas. And I don't think Laughlin was far behind! Kind of odd to be cold out here in Paradise. Kind of makes me wonder about that whole global warming thing!

I stayed up until just after midnight to welcome in the new year. I've always liked to be awake when the new year begins. **When I was a kid, I discovered that if I kept eating, it would keep me awake.** So I guess New Year's Eve is partially responsible for my shape! Not sure if I ever told you the anchovy story, but on New Year's Eve my parents would have a party and they would always serve anchovies on Ritz crackers. I used to get one to eat each year because they were **"for the adults."** Well, one year since my birthday is in January, I asked my Mom to buy me a whole can of anchovies. And on my birthday, I spread the whole can on a slice of white bread and ate it.....I was sick as a dog, and couldn't even look at an anchovy for my whole life up until a few years ago! Too much of a good thing, I guess.

This year, I really enjoyed the greetings that my friends sent me on Facebook for the new year, so I thought I would share a few of them with you. Most of my friends are not priests, so I can't read **ALL** of their messages, but there are some real gems of wisdom in what they said to me and to their other friends:

"People are so worried about what they eat between Christmas and New Year's, but really they should be worried about what they eat between New Year's and Christmas! Happy New Year!" - Craig

"Happy New Year - go crazy!" - Jared/Jacob

"Please be smart tonight and be careful. We can all have fun, but we don't need to get hurt in the process." - Jesse

"May your new year be filled with lessons and memories from the year past, and hopes and joys with each day ahead." - Charlotte

"My best piece of advice for 2011 - Remember, if

you do more of the same, you'll get more of the same." - Ses

"Make it a year filled with magic." - Brad

"Love, peace and sweet beliefs - start 2011 by informing someone that you care about them - bonus points if you reach out to repair a bridge." – Michael

"Happy New Year - Drive safe, stay out of jail, be cool, and you'll make it." - Chuck

Occasionally people have asked me where I have gotten the idea for something or other I have said in my sermon. Sometimes ideas do just come to me; sometimes they are the result of reading or listening to music or thinking about the Scripture passages. Sometimes they come from conversations with friends. Sometimes, though, they do come in more direct ways. For example, I was trying to think of something to say at the Masses for New Year's Day. I had a few ideas, but nothing seemed just right. Then, I started to get a message sent to me by quite a number of people. I got a letter from a prison inmate doing a life sentence and he enclosed a copy of a message saying that it really has been an inspiration to him. I got an email from a Extraordinary Minister of Holy Communion from my NJ parish with the identical message and a note saying how inspiring it was. More and more people were calling my attention to it. After awhile, I just gave in and am now willing to admit that I think God is conspiring to have me pass this on to you today. It is a brief mediation by a popular Protestant preacher named Chuck Swindoll and it is simply called "ATTITUDE." I offer it to you for the coming New Year 2011.

"The longer I live, the more I realize the impact of attitude on life. Attitude, to me, is more important than facts. It is more important than the past, than education, than money, than circumstances, than failures, than successes, than what other people think or say or do. It is more important than appearance, giftedness or skill. It will make or break a company....a church....a home. The remarkable thing is we have a choice every day regarding the attitude we will embrace for that day. We cannot change our past...we cannot change the fact that people will act in a certain way. We cannot change the inevitable. The only thing we can do is play on the one string we have, and that is our attitude...I am convinced that life is 10% what happens to me and 90% how I react to it. And so it is with you...we are in charge of our attitude."

God bless you in 2011 and always!

Great Friends Mike Hammer and Ben Stone with Charlie
at Magic Live!

The Epiphany of the Lord

2 January 2011

FIRST READING: Isaiah 60:1-6
PSALM: Psalm 72:1-2, 7-8, 10-13
SECOND READING: Ephesians 3:2-3, 5-6
GOSPEL: Matthew 2:1-12

As we begin this new year 2011, we all have hope and dreams, goals and expectations for the new year.

I hope you all had as memorable a Christmas as I did! The Masses were beautiful, but there were less people in Laughlin this Christmas, probably due to the economy, so we only had about 1400 worship with us at the Christmas Masses. But the really **surprising fact** is that our Christmas Collection has grown steadily in the past three years, despite the economy. In 2007, our Christmas Collection was about $6500.00; in 2008, it was about $13,500.00; in 2009, it was about $15,500.00; and we're not finished counting the collection for 2010, but so far it is OVER $18,000.00.....almost three times what it was just a few years ago! I don't talk much about money, but I have to say something about it today.....**THANK YOU! THANK YOU again!**

And I am still opening my cards and presents, but I have to tell you that I have received about a dozen fruitcakes! Two of them are made by the Trappist Monks in Gethsemane, Kentucky. And two of them are made by a group of nuns in Maine who are nicknamed **"the fruitcake nuns."** I figure that if religious people made these fruitcakes, the least I can do is eat them gratefully and religiously!

I was thinking back over the events of 2010, and I was remembering some funny things that happened to me. The one that really still makes me smile happened last summer when I was up at St. Francis in Henderson. A woman there came up to me after Mass and handed me a pen. I wasn't looking for a pen, but I took it from her and looked at it. It had an inscription on it with the name and phone number of a hair-styling salon. When I looked up at the woman, she said: **"Call me, I can do something about your hair!"** I wonder what will get said to me in 2011?

Every year at this time, we're deluged with predictions about the future.

Newspapers print predictions, people check horoscopes. Unfortunately, some of the more avid horoscope fans aren't content with checking their own, they feel obliged to check mine as well! As soon as they know the date, they give me a long knowing look and sort of sigh: "So, you're a Capricorn" and that seems to say it all. I have absolutely no use for horoscopes, ever since I saw one that cautioned me to pay more attention to my wife and children!

Man has always been fascinated by the stars, and I think that's one of the reasons behind the popularity of today's Gospel. It's been featured in innumerable works of art, it's been the subject of Christmas songs. The star attracts our attention. And tons of interesting questions are raised by today's Gospel passage: WHO WERE THE WISE MEN? HOW MANY OF THEM WERE THERE? WERE THEY REALLY KINGS? WHERE DID THEY COME FROM? WHAT LANGUAGES DID THEY SPEAK? WHAT DID THE STAR LOOK LIKE? WHY DID THEY BRING GIFTS OF GOLD, FRANKINCENSE AND MYRRH? WHAT IS MYRRH ANYWAY?

The Christmas Star has sparked many legends and has become a symbol of the whole Christmas season. There's even a beautiful story about a 4th wise man who gets lost and only finds Jesus on the way to the cross.

Over 2000 years ago, wise men set out on a journey of faith, following a star, seeking Jesus. Today, you and I follow in their footsteps on our own journeys of faith, still seeking Jesus.

Today is the FIRST SUNDAY OF 2011, a brand new year lies ahead of us. We have some 50 other Sundays and some 300+ weekdays between us and next year. Hopefully 2011 will be a year in which we seek the Lord and draw closer to Him. The star in today's Gospel rightly catches our attention, but stars don't rule our lives.

For 2011 - let us seek the Lord in His Catholic Church where we worship every week. Let us try to find His will for us and really try to do what the Lord asks.

For 2011 - let us seek the Lord in His people, resolving to be careful of their needs and their hopes; trying to live and work and study and play as people who actually care about one another.

For 2011 - let us seek the Lord in ourselves, resolving to form ourselves into the holy people the Lord calls us to be. Perhaps we might even be the stars that will lead others in our families and among our friends to God.

As we begin this new year 2011, we all have hopes and dreams, goals and expectations for the new year. Some of them are like stars, they seem so distant, so unreachable. Remember the wise men. They followed a star and it lead them right to Jesus. For this new year, follow the best of your hopes and dreams, keep looking up to God for guidance, and we too will be lead right to Jesus. And there is no other place we should rather be.

God bless you!

The Baptism of the Lord

9 January 2011

FIRST READING: Isaiah 42:1-4, 6-7
PSALM: Psalm 29:1-4, 9-10
SECOND READING: Acts 10:34-38
GOSPEL: Matthew 3:13-17

"One way or another, I intend to become a saint, and you should too!" (Father Charlie)

Another truly awesome week here in Paradise! My friends in places like snow-covered New Jersey have been sending me messages referring to Laughlin as Paradise because I keep telling them that's where I live! And even though I really do intend to spend eternity in the other Paradise **(one way or another, I intend to become a saint, and you should too!)**, our little parish here is truly a Paradise right now. Just look around at our beautiful mountains and crystal clear blue water of the mighty Colorado River! Whether you're a visitor or a local, you can't help but appreciate the grandeur of this place. And the people? Well, they are like icing on this magnificent piece of cake! We are so blessed! Never forget to thank God for letting us live or visit here! **If I were marketing Laughlin to tourists, I'd be using the slogan – "Come and visit us in Paradise!"**

Speaking of tourists, last weekend one lady leaving Mass told me that I reminded her so much of Tom Bosley from "Happy Days." I don't get that too often....although some folks have said I sounded like Andy Rooney!

As of Friday, our Christmas collection is up to over $19,715.00! Each day as I open the mail, I keep finding checks from parishioners who were away over Christmas visiting family and friends and who saved their Christmas envelope for us! A few more envelopes....and we'll top $20,000.00. All I can say once again is a huge THANK YOU! **I wonder how many pastors are as blessed as I am to have people do that?**

Speaking of other pastors, I encourage our parishioners to bring me back parish bulletins when they are traveling and visit other parishes. I'd also encourage our visitors to do the same: bring us your parish bulletins and bring ours home to your pastors. It's always fun to read what other parishes are doing and sometimes we get some great ideas from around the country because of our traveling parishioners and visitors. Keep those bulletins coming in!

One of the things that people comment on as they travel and visit other Catholic churches is how outwardly different some things are done here or other places. If you look around at Mass, you might notice people doing various things with their hands. Sometimes holding them out, sometimes holding them up, sometimes reaching out at the Our Father and joining hands with their neighbors. Some of those hand movements are imitating the movements that the priest is doing during the Mass. Sometimes priests get upset if everyone is not doing the exact same thing. **I just want you to know that as long as you don't have your hand in your neighbor's pocket, it's fine with me!** Extending our hands in prayer can be a way of showing our openness to what God is offering to us. Raising our hands up to heaven can be a sign of our offering of praise to God. Touching our hands to our chest during some of the prayers can be a sign of our seeking God's mercy. Reaching out our hands to our neighbor can be a sign of our oneness in Christ. Or sometimes keeping your hands folded can be a sign of your own prayerfulness.

Here's a little assignment for today. During the rest of the Mass, try to be aware of what you and your neighbors are doing with your hands. We don't have to all be the same. We just need to be respectful of others who might feel differently about their gestures during Mass.

And one of the things we do with our hands is to bless ourselves with holy water usually as we enter or leave a church. That holy water is a reminder of our Baptism into the Catholic Faith. Years ago, when some priest or deacon poured water over our head, he brought us into the Church. This was the beginning of our Catholic Christian life. In baptizing us, the priest or deacon represented Jesus Christ.

And at every Baptism, Jesus continues to work wonders with water. It is no less a miracle than the crossing of the Red Sea, or the changing of water into wine, or the cleansing of the whole earth at the time of Noah with the great flood, that God Himself would bring creatures like us into His kingdom for all eternity. **But that in fact is what Baptism does.** When we are baptized, we begin the process by which we will develop in the Catholic Faith and eventually, God willing, inherit eternal life with God. **Each Baptism is the beginning of an eternal miracle. And it is a step towards eternity in the real Paradise.**

All of us who have been baptized have been brought into a relationship with God that will last for all eternity. As we celebrate today the Baptism of Jesus, I just thought it would be good to remind you how fortunate we are to have been baptized. Isaiah puts it very well in today's First Reading: **"I, THE LORD, HAVE CALLED YOU; I HAVE GRASPED YOU BY THE HAND."**

Just think of that image for a moment......you and I are walking hand-in-hand with God! Doesn't that make you feel really secure? When things get really tough as they sometimes do in life, you can reach out and God's hand will be there to steady you and support you. We were talking about our hands a few moments ago. Think about that powerful image of holding hands with God.

As we continue our journey through life, may we never forget how close God has chosen to be to us. May we keep our hands safely in His throughout our lives. What began at our baptism goes on into eternity. **How fortunate we are to be holding hands with God!**

God bless you!

2nd Sunday in Ordinary Time - "A"

16 January 2011

FIRST READING: Isaiah 49:3, 5-6
PSALM: Psalm 40:2-4, 7-10
SECOND READING: 1 Corinthians 1:1-3
GOSPEL: John 1:29-34

"It will be severe. Go and collect firewood for the winter."

What an awesome week! This week included Thanksgiving, Christmas, and my birthday! Well, okay, in the real world it was just an ordinary week. But in my world....On Thursday, I was invited out by a parish family who had not been all together for Thanksgiving, so they saved a turkey and prepared an entire Thanksgiving Dinner on Thursday night! How cool is that?! Turkey and stuffing and all the fixings! **(Thanksgiving, and it wasn't even Thanksgiving!)** And then on Friday, I was surprised after the 8:00 AM Mass with a cake and candles for my birthday! One of our parishioners had arranged for the Mass intention to be for me, so I not only got to pray for myself, but got to enjoy cake with a few dozen of our weekday Mass crowd! (Actually two cakes....an apple dump cake and a cherry pie-filling cake!) My birthday isn't even until next week, but I've already had cake! **And then on**

Friday night, I had Christmas with my family. Only three of us (Michael, Eddie and me) had been together on the real Christmas, so we promised Andy that we wouldn't open presents until we could all be together, so all four of us were at the house on Friday night, went out for dinner, and then opened presents after midnight! My best gift was from Eddie who gave me a miniature OSCAR award and on the bottom is says **"BEST DAD"**. He also had his current girlfriend bake me chocolate chip cookies. That kid knows the direct route to my heart! We laughed and talked well into the morning. Welcome to my world. It's a really cool place!

Michael has a friend staying with us for a few weeks named Damron. Cool guy, but after hearing Michael and I talk and banter with each other, he finally yelled **"You two, stop talking! You're not allowed to talk to each other! Ever!"** He'll get used to us! Michael tossed me a sweat band one night and I put it on and said: **"You know, I never could understand these things! I mean, are there really people who sweat so much that that it runs down their arms into their hands and bothers them?"** So Michael starts jogging through the living room like this..... And I still couldn't understand why you put these things on your wrists! Boy, did I feel dumb when he had to explain it! Of course, I was showing him some old pictures and explained that they were small and square because they were taken by a **"Brownie"** camera. I forgot that those cameras were before his time. He said **"What?"** I said: **"Don't you know? Brownie!"** So he just yelled back at me. **"Why don't you explain it to me, Whitie?"** Maybe Damron is right..... Let me tell you a story.....

A new chief was selected to head an Indian Tribe. He was young and had never learned the "old ways" but he took his position seriously. As summer ended, the people came to him as chief and asked him if the winter was going to be severe or not. He didn't know what to answer, but he told them **"It will be severe. Go and collect firewood for the winter."** So the Indians set about collecting firewood.

As the weeks of autumn pressed on, the people came to him again and asked the same question. He told them he would answer them on the next day. Not knowing what to do, he snuck off to the general store and called the National Weather Service to ask how bad the winter was going to be. He was told that it would be very bad. So the next day, he told the Indians that they needed to collect even more firewood for the winter would be very bad.

As winter approached, the people came to him again and asked if he still felt the winter would be very bad. Again, he said he would answer them the next day, and at night he again called the National Weather Service which assured him the winter would be terrible. Again, he relayed the information to his people who set about collecting even more firewood.

In mid-December he began to doubt the severity of the winter so he again called the National Weather Service and asked them how bad the winter would be. They told him it would be awful! He wanted to know how sure they were, so he asked them **"How do you know that the winter will be so bad?"** And they replied, **"Because the Indians are collecting firewood like crazy!"**

Don't we see that same dynamic in life sometimes? Popular pollsters tell us we should feel or think a certain way, and sure enough we start thinking or feeling that way. Sometimes we just feed the frenzy without knowing what is really going on.

Today's First Reading reminds us that we're supposed to be the **LIGHT** for the nations, we're supposed to be the trendsetters for God's ways. We're supposed to be holy and influence the world by our holiness, not the other way around. In doing this, our attitude towards life is very important.

A few years ago, Chuck Swindoll, a popular Protestant preacher, wrote a brief meditation about **"ATTITUDE"** which I read at Mass on New Year's Day this year. I think it's worthwhile for all of us to hear it. Think about it during the coming weeks. Don't let what happens to you in life be more important than your attitude towards life:

"The longer I live, the more I realize the impact of attitude on life. Attitude, to me, is more important than facts. It is more important than the past, than education, than money, than circumstances, than failures, than successes, than what other people think or say or do. It is more important than appearance, giftedness or skill. It will make or break a company....a church....a home. The remarkable thing is we have a choice every day regarding the attitude we will embrace for that day. We cannot change our past...we cannot change the fact that people will act in a certain way. We cannot change the inevitable. The only thing we can do is play on the one string we have, and that is our attitude...I am convinced that life is 10% what happens to me and 90% how I react to it. And so it is with you...we are in charge of our attitude."

God bless you!

3rd Sunday in Ordinary Time - "A"

23 January 2011

FIRST READING: Isaiah 8:23 - 9:1, 6
PSALM: Psalm 27:1, 4, 13-14
SECOND READING: 1 Corinthians 1:10-13, 17
GOSPEL: Matthew 4:12-23

"If I can't be a good example, I can at least be a horrible warning!"

What an awesome week in Paradise! I know I say that a lot, but it's true! The Clergy Days this week in Palm Springs were really good! We had a great speaker on the topic of the Biblical prophets and I learned a lot from her. Got to spend some time with Father John McShane who established our parish in 1992, and got to spend some time with Father John Assalone who worked with me this past summer here and at St. Francis of Assisi in Henderson. As usual, he tried to distract me with his texting again during the sessions, but I only texted him back a few times! I was trying to be a good example. He then gave me a button which reads: **"If I can't be a good example, I can at least be a horrible warning!"**

On Wednesday, my birthday, I drove out to LA to be with Eddie and Andy. Michael couldn't make it, he had to work.

But they had a cake for me with the initial **"C"** outlined in lighted candles. I had to blow them out quickly before we set the apartment fire alarm off! Good thing they didn't light a candle for each of my 63 years! Then I went out to see them in a cool play called **"CATS AND DOGS"**. They make me so proud! Eddie introduced me as his Pa, and told the cast that he was the **"son I never wanted, but now have!"** They're still not sure what to make of that!

One afternoon, I went to Indio, and I went out to a local date farm. **I haven't had a date in years so I figured it would be fun.** It's been around for over 70 years and they show a cool tacky video with the title: **"The Romance and Sex Life of the Date"**! I learned a lot about date-growing in the Imperial Valley of California. And then I had to visit the date bar to try all the samples. I never knew there were tons of varieties of dates! After eating a few, I asked the salesgirl what the calorie count is for a date, and I was pleasantly surprised to learn that there are only 23 calories in a date, and no fat, and tons of potassium....so I ate some more of them happily and brought back a few packages of them for snacking.

I should mention that all four of us in my family are trying to get into shape this year as our New Year's resolution. And we all have **different** reasons for doing it.

Michael wants to get into top physical condition so he can do a Triathlon in a few months (running, biking, and swimming for miles!). Eddie wants to get ripped so he can attract every girl West of the Mississippi River! Andy wants to look lean and muscular so he can get a shirtless picture taken to get him more movie work. And that leaves me..... The guys got together, and Michael was their spokesman. He told me: **"Charlie, you keep talking about how you want to live and see us successful on the stage. Well, you need to be doing something to insure your health and longevity!"** So basically I was told I have to lose weight and get into shape because they want me to stay alive to be with them. **How cool is that!?!** So I'll be watching what I eat, and heading out for some walks and stuff even though it's not even Lent yet!

I don't know how it is for you, but I love to sleep in a little in the morning. I even have a little ritual about waking up in the morning. I always set my alarm for exactly 5:17 A.M. - not that I actually get up at that time, but I just like to wake up, realize that it is 5:17 A.M. and I don't have to get up yet. Then I push the **SNOOZE BUTTON** on my clock radio which gives me exactly 9 minutes more sleep. I actually enjoy those 9 minutes more than the whole night because I'm aware of having them! (Some mornings, I like them so much that I push the **SNOOZE BUTTON** 2 or 3 times more!) And I must look kind of funny when I sleep....as far back as I can remember, I've always slept with the covers pulled up over my head with just a little space for my nose. My college roommate told me years ago that I looked like a 500 year old nun!

Eventually, though, I do get up, and open my eyes. The brightness of the daylight usually hurts my eyes a little until I get used to it. It takes time to get adjusted to the light of day coming into our eyes. Somehow, I think, this also describes our experience of God. Today's readings very obviously describe God as **LIGHT**. He is Isaiah's **"LIGHT THAT SHINES IN A LAND OF GLOOM"**; He is the psalmist's **"LIGHT AND SALVATION"**; He is the Gospel's **"LIGHT THAT SHINES ON A PEOPLE LIVING IN DARKNESS."** The suggestion is clear enough - the Church wants us to think today about God as our **LIGHT**.

But God, like any light, can hurt our eyes at first. And for all of us, it is sometimes easier to just close our eyes to what God is showing us, and to enjoy the darkness of our old ways and our old habits. God's light frequently brings into view things and people that we'd really prefer not to see. Left in our darkness, we might never have seen that person in need of a ride or a kind word; that person in need of some advice that will cost us some of our time. But in God's light, that person is clearly seen. Left to ourselves, we could close our eyes to problems in our world and in our community - hunger, pain, poverty, sickness, unemployment, fear, loneliness and so many others that haunt the young and the old. But in God's light, we can see them vividly. Even our own faults and sins can hide in our darkness, but in God's light, we can see the importance of correcting them.

As we gather here to worship our God today, we should sincerely ask Him to let His light shine in our lives, to let us see ourselves as God sees us. Let us ask God to let us see the world and other people as God sees them. Just imagine what that type of vision could do for us and for our families and for our whole community! Let's try to see this world, our world, as God see it! What a difference that could make!

Like the light of morning, it might take us a little while to get adjusted to God's light, but once we get adjusted to it, we'll see that it far surpasses anything that darkness could ever offer.

God bless you!

4th Sunday in Ordinary Time - "A"

30 January 2011

FIRST READING: Zephaniah 2:3; 3:12-13
PSALM: Psalm 146:6-10
SECOND READING: 1 Corinthians 1:26-31
GOSPEL: Matthew 5:1-12

Blessed are the troublemakers - They are my beloved children and my secret agents.

I got one last birthday present this week...a huge box arrived at our house in Las Vegas. It was a package from Lance Burton. I lifted it, and shook it and tried to guess what it might contain. Michael, my brother, rolled his eyes and said, **"Just open it!"** And it was a huge basket filled with about 2 dozen different packages of cookies, nuts, cheese, crackers, and other snacks. Michael and I sat on the floor going through it like two kids in a candy store! And Michael came up with an idea. **"This is rich people's food. You and I will never be rich, but we can enjoy this tonight. We'll open each package and eat just one piece!"** So one by one, we ate cookies filled with jam, candied nuts, slices of pepperjack cheese, garlic crackers, gourmet popcorn until we had sampled everything. In hindsight, maybe it wasn't the best mixture for us late at night, but it sure was fun!

And thinking of fun, our bus trip to Las Vegas on Thursday was awesome. Nearly 60 people journeyed with me to two of my favorite magic shows, and we got a tour of our cathedral. I've been in Guardian Angel Cathedral many times, but I never knew the story of its history dating back to the 1950's when it began in the Royal Casino as a place for casino workers to have Mass at 4:30 AM on Sunday mornings when they came off their night shift. It later evolved into a shrine for tourists and casino workers, and in 1995 it became to mother church of our diocese of Las Vegas. The design and stained glass windows are so powerful and beautiful. I wonder if there were any people back in the early days who would ever have guessed what such a small beginning would grow into. God works in some amazing ways. And before we left, we gave the rector of the cathedral one of our parish casino chips. He's already emailed me and said he would be having one designed for the cathedral. I told him to just remember who came up with the idea first! Might as well get some credit!

Today's Gospel from St. Matthew is a portion of a larger section in Matthew's Gospel called **The Sermon on the Mount**. Back in 1966, when I graduated from high school, I actually used this section called **The Beatitudes** as the opening of my address as the class valedictorian. Guess I never thought I'd be preaching about it someday here in Paradise along the banks of the Colorado River! I've always loved to play with words and try to convey particular meanings through them. I guess even at a young age, I was a talker!

St. Matthew's Gospel gives us more of the words of Jesus than any of the other Gospels. Today's Gospel reminds us that we are all called to live in a way that is different from what the world considers the norm. That means that we are supposed to live in such a way that our lives influence the world around us so that people who look at the way we Catholics live can see our Faith at work and ultimately give glory to God, our heavenly Father. In the days and weeks ahead, think what that means for each of us. How can we let God's light shine more clearly through us? How can we live out more fully what Jesus says?

But in thinking about playing with words, I came across something interesting. Some writers have tried to imagine what it would be like if Satan (the devil) had a list of his beatitudes. I got to thinking about it, and played around with what others had written and think it makes a very powerful comparison with the real beatitudes we just read in today's Gospel. If what Jesus said brings us joy and eternal happiness, think about what Satan says and the problems it would bring to us.

You know, if Satan had a list of beatitudes, I think it would go something like this:

Blessed are those who are too tired, too busy, too distracted to spend an hour once a week with their fellow Catholics in church - they are my best workers!

Blessed are those who wait to be asked and expect to be thanked for everything they do - I can use them in my business.

Blessed are those who are touchy and always griping. Soon they will stop coming to church - They shall be my missionaries.

Blessed are the troublemakers - They are my beloved children and my secret agents.

Blessed are they who gossip - for they shall cause strife and divisions that please me.

Blessed are the complainers - I'm all ears to them!

Blessed are those who have no time to pray - They are already mine!

Blessed are those who profess to love God, but hate their

brothers and sisters here on earth - they will be with me forever!

Blessed are you when you hear this and think that it has everything to do with those other people and nothing to do with you - I've got room for you in my kingdom.

Scary thoughts that could have been penned by the devil himself. Worth thinking about.

But let's wrap this up with something more hopeful! Let's wrap this up with the words from St. Matthew's Gospel today that Jesus gives us in the **REAL BEATITUDES**: **"Rejoice and be glad, for your reward will be great in heaven."**

We have a lot for which we are thankful, and a lot still yet to do while we are here on earth. With God's help, we can do so much!

God bless you!

5th Sunday in Ordinary Time - "A"

6 February 2011

FIRST READING: Isaiah 58:7-10
PSALM: Psalm 112:4-9
SECOND READING: 1 Corinthians 2:1-5
GOSPEL: Matthew 5:13-16

Be salt! Be light! Be good! Be strong! Be you!

What a crazy week! Somehow I got a pinched nerve in my neck and my whole right arm and hand went limp! Giving Communion was a real issue this week! If you extended your hands, I had a chance. If you opened your mouth, I did the best I could, but some folks came dangerously close to receiving Communion in their eye! If I tried to raise my arm, it just wouldn't go where I wanted it to go! The doctor said it would go away, but since my brother, Michael, is a massage therapist, I asked him if he could do anything to help me. He told me to lay down on the floor, and he started working on my neck. Periodically, he would start laughing when he would ask me to try to do something with my arm. I asked what he was laughing at, and he told me I looked like a "deranged marionette!" He laughed so much that I asked him how much of what he was doing to me was for my benefit and how much was for his own amusement! The most memorable moment was when he started stretching my neck, and he asked me to tell him when it hurt. I innocently inquired: **"So you can stop doing it?"** and he said, **"No, so I know how to hurt you when I want to in the future!"** What he did helped a lot but the visit to the chiropractor really did the trick! Within minutes, he released the pinched nerve and I was able to use my right arm and hand again!

I'm ready for the **SuperBowl** this weekend. I have my trusty **FOOTBALL FOR DUMMIES** book handy in case I need it. Michael doesn't think I'm a REAL Steelers' fan because he saw a picture of me wearing a CHEESEHEAD. He said no REAL Steelers' fan would ever wear that! But now a good friend gave me a Troy Palomalu hat to wear, so I feel really like a true Steelers' fan!

By the way, this will be the first ever SuperBowl without CHEERLEADERS! The Steelers and the Packers have not had cheerleaders for years! There are 4 other teams in the NFL without cheerleaders: Giants, Bears, Browns and Lions. Now that's a piece of cool trivia to use at SuperBowl parties this weekend!

And then I found out about an elephant named Jenny and an orangatang named Eli who are used to predict Superbowl winners and losers! Just want to note that both the elephant and the orangatang pick the Packers to win, but I'm still sticking with the Steelers!

Well, while Steelers and Packers are the two big words this weekend, there are two other big words in our readings today that we need to pay attention to.

Salt and Light are the two big symbols in today's readings. We are called to be the **salt** and the **light** that the world needs. Do you remember a popular TV show from about 10 years ago called "ED"? It was actually filmed in Northvale NJ, right down the road from my parish. They actually needed a church to film one of their episodes, and I wanted so badly to volunteer mine, but the diocese wouldn't allow it. So they used the local Episcopalian church instead, and the minister got to play himself in that episode. I was so close to having that part! But in another episode, they had a delivery of 1000 salt shakers filled with salt. At the end of the filming, they called me and asked if I could use them. I gladly took them and put up a display of them, calling them TV show memorabilia...and then I sold them for $1 each to raise money for the parish! Just a little creativity with some extra salt!

Just a couple of thoughts about salt and light today.....

Salt was a much-valued item in the ancient world. It was a symbol of purity, it was a much-used preservative, and it was a very basic flavor-enhancer for food. Wars were fought over salt mines! When Jesus said in the Gospel

234

that we are supposed to be the **"salt of the earth"**, His listeners knew that was important. They were supposed to live exemplary lives, they were supposed to preserve the world from errors and corruption, and they were to add a particular flavor to the world. A little bit of salt goes a long way in making a difference in a meal and in a family or a community.

And in a society without electricity, light was really a cherished item. So when Jesus said in the Gospel that we are supposed to be the **"light of the world"**, people knew the value of the light and warmth of a fire or even of a single candle or oil lamp. In a dark space, even a single flame of light makes a huge difference! It dispels the darkness, it gives reassurance and hope, it takes away fears of the night. So, what does this mean for us on SuperBowl weekend in 2011?

It means that being a Christian comes with a few requirements. It means we can't just take it all for granted and feel we don't have to do anything to thank God for sharing His faith and life with us. It means we have to be willing to do what's good and right even when it is difficult or unpopular. It means we have to act in such a way that others around us can be inspired to do the same in their lives. It means that we have to bring the light of Christ to all who are in the darkness of sin or error. It means we have to flavor the world with the goodness of our faith and actions.

So this week, resolve to be creative in living your faith. Think what you can do differently that would benefit those around you in your family or in your community of friends and neighbors. Look for opportunities to bring the light of Christ to the conversations you have, to the places you visit, to the people you care about the most.

The Steelers and the Packers are going out on the field this weekend to win! And they are giving all they have to make that happen! Surely, our Catholic Faith should send us out into the world with at least as much determination and enthusiasm for what we have to offer the world of those around us. Be salt! Be light! Be good! Be strong! Be you! Because you might be the one person in the world who can reach someone that no one else can reach with the peace and the power and the love of God! Go and do it!

God bless you!

6th Sunday in Ordinary Time - "A"

13 February 2011

FIRST READING: Sirach 15:15-20
PSALM: Psalm 119:1-2, 4-5, 17-18, 33-34
SECOND READING: I Corinthians 2:6-10
GOSPEL: Matthew 5:17-37

In today's Gospel, Jesus uses some mighty strong language to reinforce His points about the importance of the spirit behind the Commandments.

Another amazing week in Paradise! Believe me, I don't say that lightly! I keep thinking that this all might be a wonderful dream and someday I will have to wake up! Besides getting an awesome haircut (and the incredibly relaxing free shampooing that comes with it here in Laughlin!), I stopped over at the local Office Max to get some printing done. The printing cost me only about $5, but by the time I left the store, I had spent nearly $60! I blame it on Domanic and Sal there! They know I love a sale so when they told me they had storage boxes (Bankers' Boxes) on sale for only $1 each, I immediately bought a few. But then I thought about it and bought 20. When they lugged them to the cashier, they mentioned that there were only 20 more left, so I ended up buying

40! And then they had rulers on sale for only 10 cents! I can always use a few rulers! **I'm definitely a sucker for a sale!**

And there's a new brewpub in town - PINTS! I'm not a big beer drinker, but they've got an incredible Beer Cheese Soup served in a huge sourdough bread bowl! And a great thing called the Blue Apple Wrapple - sliced Granny Smith apples mixed with crumbled bleu cheese and shredded lettuce, with a Raspberry vinegrette and wrapped in a wholewheat wrap, and served with a bowl of cottage cheese! It looks amazing, tastes awesome, and is totally healthy! How cool is that!?!

And I received a beautiful card from a great Jewish woman who just celebrated her 85th birthday. She was a co-worker with my Mom for many years. Lucille always refers to me as **"my priest"** which still catches the attention of her Jewish friends! In her card she wrote: **"How often I think of your Mom! And she still makes others laugh...particularly when people ask me how I keep going strong at 85. It is then I quote your Mom and reply - 'if you keep moving, they can't bury you!'"**

And when I wasn't eating or buying boxes, I was following a controversy online. Someone came out with an iPhone app called **"PENANCE"** in which you download the app and then create SAINT and SINNER accounts. Everyone starts of five HORNS as a SINNER and five HALOS as a SAINT. A horn allows a SINNER to make a confession which is randomly sent out to a dozen SAINT accounts who can then send back a PENANCE at the cost of a HALO. If the SINNER accepts the PENANCE, the SAINT is REWARDED with TWO HALOS.

Then, someone came out with another iPhone app called "**CONFESSION**". In this one, you enter your sins and other details about yourself, and it is password protected so that the sins are only linked to you. At the end of the use, it deletes your sins. And then on Wednesday, the **VATICAN** declared: **"One cannot speak in any way of confessing via iPhone!"**

It all reminded me of a **DRIVE-IN** confessional idea that a young priest once had in the days before the Internet. Of course, he ran into trouble with his pastor when he wanted to put a neon sign up over the drive-in window that said: **TOOT AND TELL OR GO TO HELL!**

And that was my week!

I took a lot of words to tell you about my amazing week here in Paradise, but Jesus uses some very important words to tell us about some of the keys to ending up in the "real" Paradise in our Gospel today. This is all part of a section of Matthew's Gospel called **"The Sermon on the Mount."** Jesus was outdoors teaching His disciples and the crowds, looking very much like Moses giving the Law to the ancient Israelites. He takes the commandments which the people truly revered, and he gets to the heart of them with His powerful words. Notice the pattern: **"You have heard that it was said.....BUT I SAY TO YOU!"**

You have heard that it was said **YOU SHALL NOT KILL, AND WHOEVER KILLS WILL BE LIABLE TO JUDGMENT,** but I say to you **WHOEVER IS ANGRY WITH HIS BROTHER WILL BE LIABLE TO JUDGMENT.**

You have heard that it was said **YOU SHALL NOT COMMIT ADULTERY,** but I say to you that anyone who even **LOOKS** at a woman with lust has already committed adultery with her.

And Jesus continues through a whole list. And suddenly those big sins **OUT THERE** become dangerously personal to us **RIGHT HERE!**

Oh, I'd never kill anyone! But wait, what about being angry with someone, even someone very close to me. Yeah, I do that! Darn, now I've got to do something about that! The Lord Himself is telling me to get rid of that attitude.

And, of course, I'd never commit adultery! But wait, haven't I sometimes looked too long and thought too much about it? Yeah, I've done that! Darn, now I've got to do something about that! The Lord Himself is telling me to even watch what I look at. And the list goes on....

And Jesus is a Master Teacher. He wants to make sure we remember His words. So he gives us a memorable word picture. **IF YOUR RIGHT EYE CAUSES YOU TO SIN, TEAR IT OUT AND THROW IT AWAY.....IF YOUR RIGHT HAND CAUSES YOU TO SIN, CUT IT OFF AND THROW IT AWAY.**

I was a high school teacher for 16 years, and when I wanted my students to remember to do something, I would tell them: **"Remember, you would rather run razor blades through your eyes than forget to do this assignment!"**

Neither the Lord nor I ever intended that our listeners would be tearing out eyes, cutting off hands, or playing with razor blades! But like my students, Jesus' disciples never forgot what the Lord had said! And neither should we!

Take some time today to think about what leads you into sin, and then resolve to work at getting rid of it, whatever it is. God promises to help you. But you have to recognize His help when it comes, and your need to be helped by it. Even God can't help get rid of sin if we keep fooling ourselves that there is no sin!

We don't need an iPhone app or the **TOOT AND TELL** idea, we just need to be honest with ourselves and with our God.

God bless you!

7th Sunday in Ordinary Time - "A"

20 February 2011

FIRST READING: Leviticus 19:1-2, 17-18
PSALM: Psalm 103:1-4, 8, 10, 12-13
SECOND READING: 1 Corinthians 3:16-23
GOSPEL: Matthew 5:38-48

Why should we try to be holy? Why should we try to love even our enemies? Because God is holy, and because God loves even those who don't love Him.

Another amazing week for me here in Paradise! While some of my single friends were struggling to find a date for Valentine's Day, I was invited out to dinner by not **ONE** but **TWO** lovely ladies! And then on Tuesday, Father Peter across the river treated me to lunch and a tour of the construction of their beautiful new church at St. Margaret Mary. On Wednesday, I ended up out for dinner in Vegas at the Palms as the guest of not **ONE**, but **TWO** magicians. And on Thursday, I was standing in line at the Riverside to go in to the cafe to use a comp from one of our parishioners and **TWO** snowbird couples came up and treated me! So I ended up with **FOUR** nights eating out with great people at no cost to me and I still have a comp left over for the cafe at the Riverside! How cool is that!?!

And I have to throw in one quick story about my brother Michael. I spent Friday night with him for his 41st birthday. At 2AM, we found ourselves talking in the living room talking about our Mom's and then about what might happen when we get old and if one of us ends up in a hospital bed unable to communicate. He assured me that he would be right there looking down at me and joking **"I know what you're thinking"** and trying to make me laugh. I assured him that if the situation were reversed, I would be right there looking down at him and reminding him of all the jokes and stories I like to tell, and retell, and retell. And without blinking an eye, he said **"Charlie, with my last ounce of strength, I would pull myself up and headbutt you into unconsciousness!"** That's my brother!

You know it's fun to speculate on situations and to discuss what people think or do. I remember hearing a great exchange between an older husband and wife. He commented to her: **"You never seem to show any anger, even when I do something that upsets you."** And she just smiled back at him, but he persisted: **"What do you do when you're angry at me?"** So she told him: **"When I get angry at you, I clean the toilet."** He had to ask: **"Why does cleaning the toilet help your anger go away?"** And she responded: **"I use your toothbrush!"**

One of the most asked questions in the world is simply **"Why?"** Why is the sky blue? Why did you say that? Why didn't you call? Why do bad things happen to good people? Why did this happen to me? Why? Why? Why?

It even happens in our religious life. Why should I try to be good? Why should I not be angry? Why should I love my neighbor and even my enemy? Why should I try to be holy?

And today's readings give us a really powerful answer!

It is extremely rare to get a Sunday where all three of the readings are perfectly aligned. But today we have one!

"Be holy, for I, the Lord, your God, am holy." - Leviticus

"You are the temple of God, and the Spirit of God dwells in you...for the temple of God which you are is holy." 1 Corinthians

"Be perfect just as your heavenly Father is perfect." St. Matthew

WHY? Because God expects us to start thinking and acting like He does!

Just think about that for a moment....God wants me to be good, to be holy, to be loving toward my neighbor and even my enemy precisely because God is good and holy and loving even toward those who don't love Him. That's what that bit in today's Gospel about the sun shining and the rain falling on the just and the unjust is all about.

God wants us to be like Him! Now that is a tall order, but it's also a great vote of confidence from our Creator. **God actually thinks we can do this!**

I suggest we start small. If we can't all-out love our enemies, maybe we can start by at least praying for them, at least asking that God would find a way to get His message through to them. It's a small start, and it might lead to a beautiful finish.

Remember: **What God thinks can become real!** And Jesus tells us to **"Be perfect, just as your heavenly Father is perfect."** God actually thinks we can do this! And so we can!

God bless you!

8th Sunday in Ordinary Time - "A"

27 February 2011

FIRST READING: Isaiah 49:14-15
PSALM: Psalm 62:2-3, 6-9
SECOND READING: 1 Corinthians 4:1-5
GOSPEL: Matthew 6:24-34

"What I do worry about during a flight is what happens if the pilot's time comes during the flight."

Another great week here in Paradise! On Friday, I was treated to three meals by three different people! Went out to breakfast at the Pioneer with a group of our church ladies and one of them paid for my breakfast. Got taken out to lunch at Harlow's by a couple preparing for the Baptism of their son. Got taken out to dinner at the Regency by a parishioner just because we like talking with each other. **This for me is a new personal record for being taken out three times in one day!** I was a little worried about watching my diet, but just for the record, I ate a salad at two out of the three meals, so I stayed pretty close to my diet!

Earlier this week, I flew out to Burbank. Sat next to a worried woman on the plane. I knew she was worried because she grabbed my hand and told me that she didn't like flying. And she was worried about this maybe being when her time would come. I reassured her that I never worry when flying. I don't worry if my time might come during a flight. She calmed down a little until I added, **"What I do worry about during a flight is what happens if the pilot's time comes during the flight."** She left me alone after that.

Worry is a very strange thing, yet we all do it. Studies indicate that we have a lot of stress and worry in our lives. We worry about ourselves, our children, our marriages, our jobs, our mortgages, our retirement, our health, our grades in school, the economy, the world situation, the end of the world, the new Mass translations coming out this fall, and so much more.

I read a cute story about a lady who was worrying about whether or not to have a facelift. But it was very expensive. As she was discussing the high cost with her husband, she said: **"But what if I drop dead three months after I have this surgery? Then what would you do?"** The husband thought for a moment and said: **"Well, I guess then we'd have an open casket for your funeral."**

Even Jesus talks about worrying, and I love to read today's Gospel where He tells us so clearly **"Do not** worry." And He gives us the example of so many things in life. Consider the birds of the air - God takes care of them. Consider the wild flowers - God takes care of them. And then He reminds us **"Are you not more important than them?...Your heavenly Father know what you need."**

Most of what we worry about, we can't do anything about. So why let it bring us down. Obviously, if we can do something about it, then go and do it...don't just whine and worry about it. But if we can't do anything about it, then we need to trust that God will get us through it. **"Do not worry"** is as close to a direct command from Jesus as we will ever see in any of the Gospels.

Maybe we need a little more of the attitude that Bobby McFerrin sang about some years ago in the song: **"Don't Worry, Be Happy!"** We sometimes laugh at that song, but the words make a lot of good sense that I suspect Jesus would agree with:

"Here is a little song I wrote. You might want to sing it note for note. Don't worry, be happy. In every life, we have some trouble, when you worry, you make it double. Don't worry, be happy."

"When you worry, your face will frown, and that will bring everybody down. Don't worry, be happy."

"Don't bring everybody down like this, don't worry it will soon pass whatever it is. Don't worry, be happy."

In last weekend's bulletin, I wrote three of my favorite thoughts about worrying. In hindsight, I should have placed them in this weekend's bulletin, but I'm not going to worry about that now! Just think about them with me for a moment today:

"Worrying does not take away tomorrow's troubles; all it takes away is today's peace."
"If I thought worrying would help, I'd do more of it!"

"Before you go to bed, give your worries to God. He's going to be up all night anyway."

As Catholics, we really do try to listen to what Our Lord says to us, and we really do try to follow His teachings. We need to constantly build up our trust in God's care for us. Today's message is clear and direct: **"Do not worry."**

God said it, I believe it, that settles it!

God bless you!

9th Sunday in Ordinary Time - "A"

6 March 2011

FIRST READING: Deuteronomy 11:18, 26-28, 32
PSALM: Psalm 31:2-4, 17, 25
SECOND READING: Romans 3:21-25, 28
GOSPEL: Matthew 7:21-27

"WHOSE ASHES?"

Another great week in Paradise! I never liked hats, but people keep giving them to me so I seem to be developing a collection of them. Got one this week that says it all: **"Another Day in Paradise!"** Some folks have said that I sound a lot like Andy Rooney, and when I talk about playing slot machines, I think they might have a point. I think that they should develop little enclosures for slot machines so the annoying person sitting next to me can't talk to me! When I play, I like to kind of "zone out" and just concentrate on the machine. But I almost always end up with someone next to me who wants to talk, or who does annoying things like tapping on his or her machine, or one who brought a little stuffed bear with him and kept rubbing his paw on the glass. Even worse are those who want to touch my machine when I'm playing it! Somehow it sounds a little rude for the priest to be saying **"Touch that again and it will be your last action with that** hand!" My prayer has now become: **"Lord, give me patience...or an untraceable handgun!"**

And this week included seeing a really good movie: **THE GRACE CARD**. It's a faith-based movie and definitely worth seeing. And my week also included a homemade lemon merangue pie! I only ate a piece, and shared the rest, but it was delicious. Have to enjoy it now...Lent is coming on Wednesday.

I was emailing a friend this week and I mentioned that this coming Wednesday is the busiest day in the whole year for a priest because it is **Ash Wednesday**. Now my friend who is 40 was raised in a non-religious home and has never practiced any religion, so I thought I should explain the obvious to him. So I wrote in my email that Ash Wednesday is the day on which most Catholics and many other Christians come to church to be marked with ashes on their foreheads at the beginning of the 40 days of Lent. I explained that the mark is sometimes in the form of a cross. I wrote about all the symbolism I could think of for why we do this. I even talked about how much scrubbing it would take to get my thumb clean afterwards. I pushed **SEND** and figured I had answered any possible questions that Ash Wednesday would bring to his mind. About an hour later, I got an email back from him with just TWO WORDS and a question mark. It simply read: **"WHOSE ASHES?"** Apparently, he was aware of the growing popularity of cremation. So I found myself emailing him again because I didn't want him thinking that I was using ashes from someone's body!

Along with each of our parish bulletins this week, I have enclosed a sheet with some thoughts about Lent. Father Michael Moore will be preaching at all our Masses next weekend so this is my chance to say a few words about observing Lent. These 40 days should be days on which we draw closer to God. Being marked with ashes on Ash Wednesday is a sign that we want to observe Lent and are planning to have these 40 days make a difference in our lives. Otherwise, just getting ashes is completely meaningless. So we need to do some thinking and planning to have a good Lent **BEFORE** we face Ash Wednesday.

I certainly encourage you to come for the Lenten Mission that Father Michael Moore will be giving here. He will tell you more about it next weekend, but I will tell you now that he is an inspired priest who will captivate you with his Irish wit and wisdom. And Deacon Dan will be conducting our Stations of the Cross on each Friday of Lent at 6:00 PM followed by a meatless soup supper.

On Monday, March 21st, Dr. Stan Casebere will be presenting a talk on the Physiology of the Crucifixion. It is a beautiful and meditative reflection on the Shroud of Turin and the sufferings of Jesus Christ.

We all know that we have completely meatless Fridays in Lent, so for 6 Fridays and Ash Wednesday, we Catholics give up eating meat as a reminder of the sufferings of Christ. And on Ash Wednesday and Good Friday, we limit even the amount of food we each to one main meal and a couple of snacks. This is known as fasting. I remember as a child when EVERY Friday was meatless and my Mom would sometimes make boiled potatoes and sour cream as our Friday night dinner. Now we have great options such as pizza so it's not total suffering just a reminder that something important happened when Christ died for us.

We have special celebrations for St. Patrick's Day on March 17th, for the Feast of St. Joseph on March 19th, and for the prayerful Day of the Unborn Child on March 25th.

My personal favorite Lenten activities are our annual **LENTEN WEIGH-IN** and our **TIGER MASSES**. Stop by the church office to weigh in this week on or before Ash Wednesday, and then update your weight each week. No prizes, but one of us will be the biggest loser in Laughlin! And our Tiger Masses are at 6:00 AM each Friday of Lent. You have to be **"tough as a tiger"** to get to church that early!

Some people give up things for Lent, some people do something extra for Lent. No one does **EVERYTHING,** but we all should do something to make these 40 days a time of grace and growth for ourselves and those around us. **Just remember: It doesn't matter one bit WHAT you do for Lent. But it does matter a WHOLE LOT that you do something to make these 40 days of Lent a special time!** Like Moses' words in our first reading today, and Jesus' words in the Gospel, it's all about making choices. We need to decide what we're going to do so Lent doesn't slip past us.

Take home the bulletins and the Lenten sheets and start planning what you will be doing for Lent this year. And when you receive ashes on Ash Wednesday, let it be the beginning of a great Lent, a great change, a great time in your life.

God bless you!

First Sunday of Lent - "A"

13 March 2011

FIRST READING: Genesis 2:7-9, 3:1-7
PSALM: Psalm 51:3-6, 12-13, 17
SECOND READING: Romans 5:12-19
GOSPEL: Matthew 4:1-11

Father Michael Moore preached at all the Masses this weekend in preparation for the Lenten Retreat.

Steve and Charlie posing for the Photographer

Second Sunday of Lent - "A"

20 March 2011

FIRST READING: Genesis 12:1-4
PSALM: Psalm 33:4-5, 18-20, 22
SECOND READING: 2 Timothy 1:8-10
GOSPEL: Matthew 17:1-9

RAD...TIGHT...COOL...CHILL...WICKED... SICK...SWEET....DOPE

Another great week in Paradise! Thanks to Father Michael Moore being here, we had an inspirational Lenten Mission. Almost 200 people a day attended the four-day event. And Father Michael is very thankful for the nearly $6500 donated to the work of the St. Patrick's Fathers. He is a wonderful priest and speaker, and a great houseguest. He even made coffee for me one morning!

I got a great present in the mail. A **14" dagger** used by my sideshow friend Ses Carny. In his act, he would swallow it and then remove it. After a recent injury with it, he decided to remove it from his act! He said he wanted me to have it for my collection of sideshow items. It's a great addition and goes well with the **bed of nails** I got from him last year! He said he had an interested encounter at the post office in Massachusetts when he was mailing it to me. The clerk asked if the package contained anything hazardous or dangerous. He said **"No, it's just a dagger!"** And then looking at the address, the clerk said **"Why on earth are you mailing a dagger to a Catholic Priest?"** And he calmly replied, **"It's a long story!"** By the way, it arrived in an old sock and I asked him why he would keep such a great item in an old sock and he told me it is an old sideshow technique. If the dagger has any nicks in it, they will catch on the sock. It's better to know that **BEFORE** you try to swallow it than to find out while it's in your throat!

And thinking of my throat, you know I love to play with words in preaching, in speaking, in writing. What do you think all of the following words have in common?

RAD...TIGHT...COOL...CHILL...WICKED...SICK...S WEET....DOPE

They all currently mean the **SAME THING**! It just depends on how old you are and where you live! I can see myself using most of them really easily! "Wow, that buffet is really **SWEET**!" ... "How **COOL** is that?" ... "Check out that truck, really **CHILL**!" ... "Man, your comedy is **SICK**!" ... "Those boots are **RAD**!" ... "Real **TIGHT** hanging out with you tonight!" "That car is **WICKED**!" I still have some trouble with **DOPE**. In my generation, **DOPE** meant drugs, bad drugs. Now when

Eddie says "That show is **DOPE**!" I kind of know I'm going to like it! Wonder if anyone will ever come up to me after Mass and say **"Hey, Father, that sermon was really DOPE today!"**

Speaking of Eddie, Andy and Eddie are enjoying living in Burbank, California, but we were talking about the weird possibility of radiation reaching our West Coast from the tragedy in Japan. Andy assured me they would be okay. He said that if the radiation were approaching, he would just get in his car and drive **WEST** to avoid it. **Apparently they are not teaching geography in the schools any more!**

With the current situation in Japan because of the earthquake, tsunami, and fear of nuclear meltdown, and with the continuing unrest in the Middle East, and with our own economic problems right here in the USA, it's sometimes very easy to get scared and worry about what the future might hold for our world, for our nation, for our families and for ourselves.

The people that the Catholic Church puts before us in the readings for this Second Sunday of Lent had great concerns about the future and they too had to trust the Lord and they turned to the Lord in prayer. The future must really have been scary for them. **ABRAHAM** was told by God to leave his homeland and his kinfolk and go to a strange land....**and let's not forget that Abraham was 75 years old when he was told to uproot himself!** People who say that they're too old for anything should think of the example of Abraham. He must have wondered what would happen to him and his family, but he went as God directed him.

TIMOTHY must have wondered many times in his life what **PAUL** meant by this holy life to which God has called him as he worked with the young and struggling Christian communities to which he had been sent. There was no road map to follow. They were just starting out.
And **PETER, JAMES and JOHN** must never have forgotten their mountaintop experience as Jesus was transfigured before them and then spoke to them about **"rising from the dead"**. They must have wondered many times what the future would hold for them. And if they had our vocabulary, that mountaintop experience with Jesus must have been one **SWEET, SICK, CHILL, RAD, COOL, TIGHT, WICKED, DOPE** experience! They certainly never ever forgot it!

What do all these people have in common? **ABRAHAM, TIMOTHY, PAUL, PETER, JAMES and JOHN all had to learn to TRUST in God about an uncertain future.** And that is one of the lessons we need to learn even today as we continue our sometimes bumpy journey through life and through this holy season of Lent. We must learn to put aside our worries, our anxieties, our fears, and sometimes even our plans for the future as we learn day by day to trust in the Lord. **IT WASN'T EASY for the people in the Bible, and it probably won't always be easy for us. But they learned to do it, and so can we.**

You've heard me say it many times before, but believe me it is worth repeating today: **"We don't know what the future holds, but we know Who holds the future."** And sometimes that's all we've got to hold on to. So we had better hold on to it tightly because the ride can get bumpy and scary sometimes. Lent is a good time to recognize our need to trust God even when we don't have all the answers. And that, folks, is something really **SWEET** to hold onto!

God bless you!

264

Third Sunday of Lent - "A"

27 March 2011

FIRST READING: Exodus 17:3-7
PSALM: Psalm 95:1-2, 6-9
SECOND READING: Romans 5:1-2, 5-8
GOSPEL: John 4:5-42

"Oh great, now the two of you have a God complex!"

Another amazing week here in Paradise! Got treated to an awesome dinner with some friends on last Saturday night, a perfect piece of blackened salmon. Then got taken to brunch last Sunday and ate some more amazing seafood with friends. Thank goodness, this is Lent and I'm walking my 3 miles each day! So far, I've walked 54 miles since Ash Wednesday! And so far, in Lent, our parish weigh-in group is down over 20 pounds since we began.

Up in Vegas, I won over $600 on a Wizard of Oz machine on Monday, but for some reason the woman next to me wasn't really happy for me. She just would look over at me and say **"You got another bonus?!"** And I have to tell you how thrilled I am that you all listen to me when I preach. A few weeks ago, I mentioned how annoying it is when someone sits next to me at a slot machine and touches my machine. So many of you have seen me playing and have come over lately and tapped on the machine saying **"Is this what you don't like people doing?"** and then walk away laughing!

I went bowling late one night with Michael and 3 younger actors/singers from a touring show. Hate to be embarrassed by younger guys, so I managed to beat all of them in one game of bowling. Usually I can only beat bowlers who have been drinking, but this time, they were all sober, so it was a real win for me!

And at the Italian restaurant in the Colorado Belle, on Thursday nights, they have a deal where after dinner the manager comes over and flips you for the check. I was there on Thursday night with some friends and we racked up a nearly $70 bill. I knew it was my lucky week, so I called the coin toss (HEADS) and I won! Life is good here in Paradise!

And Eddie got two auditions in California on Wednesday. He auditioned for the role of Jesus in a new film. I am so hoping he gets the part. Since I think of Eddie as my son, that would make me the father of Jesus! He also auditioned that same day for the role of an evil drug dealer. Yeah, it would be cool if he got that one, but I like the Jesus one better! My brother Michael's take on the Jesus audition was: **"Oh great, now the two of you**

have a God complex!" That should give us some interesting conversations.

And on a very happy personal note, on Monday at 5:00 PM, the very first book I have ever published went national on Amazon.com. Details are in the bulletin, and, of course, it will be here next weekend at a discount price (I love a bargain!). And it's all about our life here in Paradise! So this is my very first time preaching to you as a published author! Never thought that would ever happen!

And that was my week....I know I do a lot of talking (It's sort of an occupational hazard), and in the course of His earthly ministry, Jesus did a lot of talking with people....not only talking to them, but talking with them. And fortunately some of the Gospels give us glimpses into these conversations with Jesus. **Matthew's Gospel, by the way, gives us more of the words of Jesus than any of the other Gospels.** Today's Gospel gives us the conversation between Jesus and a woman at a well in Samaria. I'd suggest that this conversation is important...not only to the Samaritan woman, but also to us. It is preserved precisely so we could listen in on it, and learn from it. Here we see Jesus at work drawing a person away from sin and back to Himself.

First, he asks the woman for help: **"Give me a drink."** She is startled that He even spoke to her. Then He starts from the situation (she is there drawing water from a well) and begins to explain to her that her thirst for water is just a physical expression of a much greater thirst, a thirst for God. He offers the gift of living water to her.

She responds by asking Him for help: **"Give me this water."** (A reversal) and Jesus continues talking with her. He doesn't condemn her life (she is living with a man who is not her husband, in fact, he is the 5th person she has lived with sinfully since her husband), but Jesus does remind her of her situation. Not unexpectedly, she immediately changes the subject. And she asks Jesus **"Where is the place where we should worship?"** And Jesus lets her go off on this tangent for awhile, but then brings her back to the situation at hand. **"The messiah? I Who speak with you am He."**

And the woman goes off and proclaims to all the townspeople that she has seen the Messiah, the Savior. And they go out to hear Jesus for themselves.

And they come back to her with words that would make any priest or religious educator thrilled beyond comparison: **"No longer does our faith depend on your story. We have heard for ourselves and we know that this really is the savior of the world."**

What do we learn from this Gospel? Jesus accepts each person exactly where he or she is, right in their home locality, even in the midst of their sins.

Jesus then invites each person to listen to Him and to share with Him. He sometimes even asks our help, but eventually He entices us to ask for His help in our lives.

Jesus is intent on each one of us. In the Gospel, Jesus even gave up eating with His disciples in order to spend time with this woman.

And for those of us who teach, or preach or even write books, it is good to note that Jesus did not require a Ph.D. in Religious Studies or a degree in Scripture Studies before He promised His gift of life to the woman. **All she had to do was to respond to Him in faith.**

The Samaritan woman is nameless in the Gospel. She stands for each one of us. We are accepted by Jesus right where we are, just as we are. And we are invited by Jesus to share with Him in His gift of eternal life. As this holy season of Lent progresses, we might want to think how well we respond when Jesus converses with us. Do we listen to Him? Do we enjoy our conversations (prayers) with Him? Do we make time in our lives to spend with Him? A good thought to take home with you today might be: **"If you are too busy to pray, then you are just too busy!"**

God bless you!

Fourth Sunday of Lent - "A"

3 April 2011

FIRST READING: 1 Samuel 16:6-7, 10-13
PSALM: Psalm 23:1-6
SECOND READING: Ephesians 5:8-14
GOSPEL: John 9:1-41

"Live as children of light." (St. Paul)

Another awesome week here in Paradise! A thousand copies of my newly-published book arrived on Monday and people started buying them as soon as we unpacked some of them! I'm still amazed that people actually want me to sign the books they buy! Why would anyone want my sloppy handwriting on a perfectly good new book? I really should have paid more attention to my grade school penmanship class! I remember my 4th grade teacher, Sister Teresa Aloysia, telling me that I could become a doctor. I said: **"Because I'm so smart?"** And she calmly said: **"Because you write so poorly!"**

On Tuesday, I had to attend a Risk Management Seminar in Las Vegas sponsored by our diocese. It was mandatory attendance. So my secretary, Waunita, and I had to go to it. We heard a lot about protecting the assets of the church, and it was pretty dry material. Fortunately,

Father John was sitting at the same table so he and I could share some knowing smiles as the presenters talked on. I purposely left my cellphone in my car so he couldn't text me and make me laugh and get into trouble! But the best part of the presentation was learning what we **CANNOT** do to raise money in the parish.

Over the years, I've learned that whenever someone forbids you to do something, there must have been some incident that happened to cause them to forbid you to do it. So it was fun trying to visualize what might have happened to cause the diocese to forbid us to raise funds for our parishes by any of the following methods: We cannot run **BINGO** (and I thought that was the Catholic game!); we cannot have a **DUNK-TANK** at any parish event; and we cannot use a **CHAINSAW** as part of any parish festival or recreational activity! I keep trying to visualize what some priest must have done with a chainsaw at a recreational activity to cause that particular prohibition!

On Wednesday, I helped Father John hear confessions up at St. Francis for several hours. They actually had a whole day of hearing confessions from 8AM until 5:30 PM.

With over 5000 families in the parish, they need a lot more time than our 15 minutes before each Mass here.

And at home, my brother Michael was in rare form. He and I have more fun than any two guys I know! He threw me out of the kitchen and created an awesome whole wheat pasta with spinach and mushrooms and bacon in a garlic/lemon sauce. And then we spent a few hours talking. He asked me why for the past few weeks I have started to say **"Over there"** a lot in my conversations. I told him that I didn't even know I was doing that. He said it began a few weeks ago and that I do it all the time now. Well, that made me think, so I asked him if there was anything else that I said a lot. And all he said was: **"Do you mean particular phrases, or just the sheer amount of words you always use?"**

I told him that I hoped I never go **BLIND** because I would miss seeing so much of his sarcasm! **His eyes light up when he's mocking me!** And he gets this weird smile on his face! So he said, it might be worse if I went **DEAF** and couldn't hear him. I thought about it and said I would rather be **DEAF** and not hear him, than **BLIND** and not see him when he's joking. Then he added: **"Suppose you went both DEAF and BLIND!"** I said that would be awful. But he reassured me that he would be right next to me and he would keep poking me so I would know he was there. Now that would really be annoying! And, of course, for the rest of the day, every time he got near me, he kept poking me! He certainly can be my very annoying younger brother!

And that thought of blindness brings us to today's Gospel.....

Each of us today is in one way or another limited and blind, just like the blind man in today's Gospel. And each of us also is limited and blind just like the religious leaders who persecuted the blind man and even the Lord Himself.

We either don't see the needs of the people around us, people who are in own families or neighbors, or we see them only in a garbled way. We don't always see the evils that are being done and therefore we don't always try to correct them. And we don't always see the tremendous good that people are doing and then praise and encourage them. Sometimes, each one of us, suffers from a blindness that keeps us closed in our own little world.

Just take a moment and close your eyes, both of them. Feel how dark and uncomfortable that feels. Even those among you who are trying your best to work along with me on this are already hoping to open your eyes quickly, or to at least sneak a peek to see what's going on around you. We don't like to be in darkness. And that is good.

As we move towards Easter, the symbol of light comes to our attention more and more. St. Paul tells us today that we are **"light in the Lord"** and then he adds with some emphasis: **"Live as children of light."** Light produces every kind of goodness and justice and truth. Learn what pleases the Lord and do it.

We pray that as we move through the remaining days of this season of Lent, that we may be drawn more and more into the light of Christ, that we may be healed of any remaining blindness to our sins, and that we may be enlightened by Christ and so let His light shine through us. We need to let God's light shine in our lives so we can see this world as God sees it and act accordingly.

I hope whatever you're doing to make this season of Lent a time of grace and growth is working for you. There are only a few weeks left before we get to Easter. Maybe by then I'll find out what problems a chainsaw can cause at a parish event!

God bless you.

276

Fifth Sunday of Lent - "A"

10 April 2011

FIRST READING: Ezekiel 37:12-14
PSALM: Psalm 130:1-8
SECOND READING: Romans 8:8-11
GOSPEL: John 11:1-45

"We only have one rule in heaven: Don't step on the ducks!"

Another amazing week in Paradise! I think I've signed my name more this week than ever before in my life! With all the books I've signed, I'm half-expecting to see them show up on eBay someday! And speaking of books, a lady came in to the office this week wanting to buy my book. She said that if she liked it, she would buy several more for her family and friends. But then she continued that if she didn't like it, she would want her money back! All I could think of was the recent Charlie Sheen roadtour show that got booed in Detroit, and when the people wanted their money back, the show producers said **"We just told you there would be a show. We didn't say you would enjoy it!"** So no refunds on the book! Oh, by the way, she did enjoy it and wants to buy some more!

Enjoyed one of my all-time favorite sandwiches again this week - a blue apple wrapple! Diced tart apples mixed with lettuce, walnuts and bleu cheese in a whole wheat wrap with a raspberry vinegrette dressing! Ah, that and a bread bowl of thick beer-cheese soup just makes me smile as I sit along the beautiful Colorado River. Even after a few years of being here, I still thank God every day that I get to live in Paradise! And that all of you get to live here or visit here with me.

And in emptying some more of my tons of boxes from New Jersey, I found a great old story that I'd like to share with you today.

Three women die together in an auto accident and go to heaven. When they get there, St. Peter says: **"We only have one rule in heaven: Don't step on the ducks!"** So they enter heaven, and sure enough, there are ducks all over the place. It is almost impossible not to step on a duck. Although they try their very best to avoid them, the first woman accidentally steps on a duck. Along comes St. Peter with the ugliest man she ever saw. St. Peter chains them together and says: **"Your punishment for stepping on a duck is to spend eternity chained to this ugly man!"** The next day, the second woman accidentally steps on a duck, and along comes St. Peter and with him is another extremely ugly man. He chains them together for eternity as well. The third woman has observed all this and not wanting to be chained for all eternity to an ugly man, she is **VERY** careful where she steps. She manages to go several months without stepping on any ducks. Then one day, St. Peter comes up to her with the most handsome man she has ever seen - very tan, tall, muscular, sexy. St. Peter chains them together without saying a word. The woman remarks: **"I wonder what I did to deserve being chained to you for all eternity?"** The guy looks at her and says: **"I don't know about you, lady, but I stepped on a duck!"**

I love statistics! I love playing around with numbers! I love counting down or counting up to events. I like noting things like the fact that last weekend I celebrated Mass for the 18,397th time! With that in mind, I'm sure you've all heard statistics like: 4 out of 5 doctors recommend; 8 out of 10 dentists recommend...we've all heard our share of statistics. Personally, I love the statistic that tell us that 1 out of 3 people are ugly. So if you look at the person on your right, then at the person on your left, and they look kind of normal.....

Actually, if you asked the person on your right and the person on your left: **"What do you think is the most impressive and important part of today's Gospel?"** I'm sure that 9 out of 10 people would describe the scene of Jesus raising Lazarus from the dead and bringing him out of the tomb.

I'd like to suggest something else as being the most significant part: **the scene with MARTHA and JESUS.** MARTHA has been mourning her brother's death and then Jesus says: **"Your brother will rise again."** And MARTHA says: **"I know he will rise again in the resurrection on the last day."** Then Jesus says: **"I am the resurrection and the life, whoever believes in Me though he should die, will come to life; and whoever is alive and believes in Me will never die......Do you believe this?".....**"YES, LORD, I HAVE COME TO BELIEVE THAT YOU ARE THE MESSIAH, THE SON OF GOD WHO IS TO COME INTO THE WORLD."**

Jesus led Martha from a belief in the resurrection on the last day to a faith in Him as the resurrection and the life for all who believe **RIGHT HERE and RIGHT NOW.** Where do we stand on this? Do we really believe that God is with us no matter what happens **RIGHT HERE and RIGHT NOW?**

Today's First Reading from Ezekiel reminds us: **"I will put My Spirit in you that you may live, I have promised and I will do it."**

St. Paul's Letter to the Romans reminds us: **"The Spirit of God dwells in you."** RIGHT HERE and RIGHT NOW, in the midst of uncertainty and doubt, in the midst of pain and confusion, in the midst of joy and excitement, in the midst of whatever is going on in our varied lives, God is leading us to life. **Jesus promises that He is our life now.**

And so many of us are like that third woman in the duck story. We miss the meaning of what is happening in our lives right here and right now!

In these final weeks of Lent, we should pray and work to appreciate God's presence in our world not only as a promise for some distant future, but in our very lives as the One Who gives meaning to us in the present. God shares His life and presence with us every day. I can't give you any better message to take with you from church today. **God is with us RIGHT HERE and RIGHT NOW!**

God bless you!

Palm Sunday

17 April 2011

FIRST READING: Isaiah 50:4-7
PSALM: Psalm 22:8-9, 17-20, 23-24
SECOND READING: Philippians 2:6-11
GOSPEL: Matthew 26:14 - 27:66

There is no sermon preached on Palm (Passion) Sunday. The reading of the Passion Account is more powerful than any sermon ever could be!

Easter Sunday

24 April 2011

FIRST READING: Acts 10:34, 37-43
PSALM: Psalm: 118:1-2, 16-17, 22-23
SECOND READING: Colossians 3:1-4
GOSPEL: John 20:1-9

May God bless us all on Easter with a real sense of hope for the future!

I'd like to start with a bit of history. You may have wondered about Easter being so late this year. For those of you who are curious, the date of Easter is determined more by astronomy than by the church. The **Council of Nicea** in 325 determined that we should have a date for Easter for all Christians around the world to celebrate, and they chose the date based on a lunar calendar. So Easter will always fall on the **FIRST SUNDAY** after the **FIRST FULL MOON** after the **SPRING EQUINOX** which occurs on or about March 21st. In reality, the earliest possible date for Easter is **March 22nd**, but this is very rare, which will not occur again until Easter in the year **2285**! And the latest possible date for Easter is **April 25th**, just one day later than Easter is this year, and that won't occur until Easter in the year **2038**. (By the way, I'm hoping to be around for that one!).

Interestingly enough, the most frequent date on which Easter falls throughout the centuries is April 19th, so we should all see a few of those in our lifetimes.

And a little bit about my favorite Easter treat - **PEEPS**. **PEEPS** are to Easter what fruitcakes are to Christmas! Some people love them (me!) and some people can't understand those of us who love them! But they sure are popular! Americans will eat more than 600 million **PEEPS** this Easter! And each **PEEP** has only 32 calories and absolutely no fat! People like to eat them fresh, stale, microwaved, frozen, and even as a weird topping on pizza! So if you get any **PEEPS** that you don't want, my office door will be open! By the way, if you are looking for a fun game with **PEEPS**, try **"PEEP JOUSTING"**! It's a game in which two **PEEPS** are placed in a microwave with a few toothpicks stuck in each one. As the **PEEPS** expand, one toothpicks the other, and the owner of the winning **PEEPS** gets to eat both of them! I love that game!

And, of course, it wouldn't be Easter for me unless I had a bunny. When my Mom was alive, she gave me one every Easter, and a few of my friends have kept up the tradition. This Easter, I got two awesome bunnies! One came all the way from New Jersey, and the other one came from just across the Colorado River in Arizona. I'm hoping they don't start reproducing! But they sure are cute!

This is my third Easter in Paradise! And it just keeps getting better and better here in Laughlin! If you live here, you know exactly what I mean! If you are visiting here for Easter, I hope you will have such a great time with us that you will go home knowing exactly what I mean! But Easter is more than just another day in Paradise! Easter is a wonderful celebration of hope.

Of all the celebrations that we have in our Catholic Christian Faith, Easter is by far the most powerful one. Easter reminds us each and every year that death is not the end of life. Because Jesus rose from the dead, we have the hope of eternal life.

Catholics worship God at Mass each and every Sunday throughout the year, so it is nothing new for us to be at Mass on Easter Sunday. In fact, it is exactly where we Catholics want and need to be. Some commentaries speak of each Sunday as being a **"little Easter"** so when the **"BIG EASTER"** comes along once each year, we are ready to really celebrate it! **Remember, it is not God Who benefits from our worship, it is all of us who benefit from having a right relationship with God.**

And if there is one word that springs to my mind each Easter Sunday, that word is **"HOPE"**. Because of Easter, we can hope for eternal life. If Jesus had not risen from the dead, what would we ever have to hope for beyond the years (few or many) that we're given in this life? But because of Jesus' Resurrection, we know that life has endless (eternal) possibilities! We know that life transcends time and space. We know that we are linked, connected, and in harmony with all those faithful people who have gone before us into eternal life. And we know that we will always be linked, connected, and in harmony with all those faithful people who will come after us here in Laughlin and Bullhead City and Searchlight and Kingman and Golden Valley and Fort Mohave and Needles and all the other places in God's beautiful world.

May God bless us all on Easter with a real sense of hope for the future!

As St. Augustine so wisely said so many years ago: "We are Easter people, and Alleluia is our song!"

From all of us here in Paradise to all of you here with us today, Happy Easter!

God bless you!

I know this is an Easter Sermon, but I have this great
picture of
myself with one of our parish deacons, Dan McHugh!

Second Sunday of Easter - Divine Mercy Sunday – Bright Sunday

1 May 2011

FIRST READING: Acts 2:42-47
PSALM: Psalm 118: 2-4, 13-15, 22-24
SECOND READING: 1 Peter 1:3-9
GOSPEL: John 20:19-31

"If you can make your people smile even a little bit when they come to Mass, do it! They've had a hard week, and it is good for them to laugh in church!" (Bishop Robert Morneau)

A number of years ago, back in New Jersey, I attended a workshop for priests given by Bishop Robert Morneau of the Diocese of Green Bay, Wisconsin. After a few comments about the Packers, he told us the best bit of advice any bishop has ever given me about preaching. He said: **"If you can make your people smile even a little bit when they come to Mass, do it! They've had a hard week, and it is good for them to laugh in church!"** I think you realize that I have tried really hard to always follow his advice even though I'm a Steelers' fan! That's why I tell you about my life, my family, my week here in Paradise. We all have stories to share. I'm just fortunate enough to have a built-in audience each week!

Easter Week has been awesome here in Paradise! We have nearly 1600 people celebrating Easter with us at our Masses last weekend, and our Easter Collection so far exceeds $11,000.00 so we are very grateful for the support. On Holy Saturday, I got to receive three men into our Catholic Faith, and to administer the Sacrament of Confirmation to them. So Ben and Tom and Charles now join the very small group of people who have been confirmed by me. Trust me, that is the closest I will ever come to being a bishop! After my mention of loving PEEPS so much, two children opened their Easter baskets after the Easter Egg Hunt on Sunday morning, and GAVE me the packages of PEEPS they had received! For kids to do that, on their own, really makes me so happy not only because I got two packages of PEEPS, but because they really had listened to my sermon! It just keeps getting better and better here!

And I went out to buy a vacuum cleaner. Got a great deal on a **DIRT DEVIL** over at BigLots. It was only $49.00! And with tax it came to **$53.34**. I gave the clerk three 20's, and she looked at the cash register for the amount of change, and it was **$6.66**. She was surprised, and she knows I'm a priest, so she said: **"666....isn't that evil?"** And I responded, **"Well, after all, it is a Dirt Devil!"**

And I am having a real blast at RiverRun! In conjunction with the Pioneer, we ran a sideshow event on Wednesday night that raised over $2100 for the Colorado River Food Bank! It was a lot of fun. And one of the performers raffled off a bayonet that he used to swallow. It was the next-to-last item that he ever swallowed, and he had already given me the very last item he had swallowed - a dagger. So he held it up to auction it, and swayed it in front of me and said: **"Charlie, you could have a set!"** So the bidding started, and got up to over $100 - all for the food bank! And two people were bidding against me! Until finally, JoAnn said, **"Will you stop bidding up the price! I'm buying it for you!"** So the food bank got the money, and I got the bayonet!

Been down at River Run each night and found a new treat. One of the stands is selling **CHOCOLATE-COVERED BACON!** And it really is awesome! Bacon and chocolate...two of my favorite foods....together at last!

And this weekend, Pope John Paul II is being beatified in Rome. Just a few years after his death, he is already on the quick path to being declared a saint. He was pope for over 25 years, and a truly remarkable and holy man! I was this close to him in 1995 when he came to New Jersey for Mass at Giants Stadium! **He had his back to me....but I was this close!** It poured rain the whole time he was in New Jersey, and I had placed a plastic garbage bag over my head to try to stay dry during the outdoor Mass...and wouldn't you know, the camera panned the priests and I showed up on the gigantitron screen wrapped in a plastic garbage bag for all the world to see. Years later, when the Pope met the archbishop of Newark, he commented: **"New Jersey....it always rains in New Jersey!"**

There are many names for the Sunday after Easter. At various times and in various places, it has been called **LOW SUNDAY** (because of the drop in attendance compared with Easter); the **SUNDAY IN WHITE** (because the newly-baptized used to wear their white garments to Mass for the Sunday following Easter); **DIVINE MERCY SUNDAY** (in honor of the celebration of Jesus' mercy to all of us). But my personal favorite has always been an old medieval tradition of calling this **BRIGHT SUNDAY**, a day on which we renew our **EASTER JOY**. We, as faithful Catholic Christians, can laugh in triumph over the devil. We can laugh at him because Jesus is the ultimate winner in this life and in eternal life. And because of our baptism, you and I are associated with Jesus for all time and eternity.

There's a lot going on in our lives and in our world, but God is with us through it all. Like Thomas, in our Gospel today, we sometimes need the re-assurance of Jesus. And Jesus gives it to us. And even when we fail, God's mercy is boundless and undeservedly generous. God doesn't treat us the way we deserve. He treats us the way He sees us. We all need God's mercy. Think of how merciful God has been to you....and then try to imitate God's mercy with each other!

I hope I've fulfilled Bishop Morneau's advice and made you smile a little today. Of all the people in the world, you and I are truly blessed because of our Faith, and because of our connection with our God. For reasons sometimes known only to Him, God loves us and wants only the best for us. Now that is something to smile about and to celebrate on Divine Mercy Sunday!

God bless you!

Third Sunday of Easter - "A" - Mother's Day

8 May 2011

FIRST READING: Acts 2:14, 22-33
PSALM: Psalm 16:1-2, 5, 7-11
SECOND READING: 1 Peter 1:17-21
GOSPEL: Luke 24:13-35

"Because you'll never have to share him with another woman!"

This really has nothing to do with the sermon today, but I am really happy about announcing it. As most locals know, I have been looking to buy my own house here in Laughlin for the past several years. **After all, to me this is Paradise, so I need to make sure I have my own place in Paradise.** I always talk so much about loving Laughlin, so I really needed to put my money where my mouth is! I have wanted to find a house with incredible views, but never could find the right mix of house, views and price. Well, this past weekend, a new community opened here in Laughlin at 10:00 AM last Saturday (April 30th). I was on their doorstep at 10:00 AM! And I liked the house they were building, and I loved the view from one of the lots available, and I was able to envision a VA loan to help me make the purchase, so by 2:00 PM, I was the very first buyer in the new community, just up the road from our church. When I was picking out colors, the exterior paint color that caught my attention was a light tan and the name of the color was **SUPERNATURAL**! So how cool is that? **My house is going to be built in Paradise and its exterior walls will be SUPERNATURAL!**

I was going to keep quiet about this until the house was partially built, but a local radio talk show host mentioned it on his show earlier this week and also plugged my book! So the rumor is true! Father Charlie is on his way to becoming a Laughlin homeowner! **And just for the record.....no church funds are involved in this! And there will be no second collections to pay my mortgage!** And I'm thrilled about it! My Mom loved Laughlin so I think it's kind of perfect for me to be announcing this on Mother's Day Weekend!

Happy Mother's Day to all our mothers, Godmothers, grandmothers, great-grandmothers, fostermothers, step-mothers, and other mother-like women in our lives.

I've listed a few quotes about mothers in today's bulletin because it's good for all of us to think of our mothers today. And if I have one wish for all of you in the church today, it's that you are as happy thinking about your Mom as I am thinking about my Mom. She put up with me for 58 years (not counting the 9 months before birth!) And even when the alzheimer's made her forget me sometimes, she still talked to me about her son the priest. And even at 93, she still loved to go out to eat! And she would tell me **"My son would love this place."** And I would assure her that he most certainly would love it. My memories today are golden treasures, and I hope yours are too! When I was ordained, one of Mom's friends told her that she was so fortunate to have a son become a priest. When Mom asked WHY, the friend replied **"Because you'll never have to share him with another woman!"** Mom kind of liked that a lot!

And so we move from mothers to wives.....

Three men were sitting together bragging about how they had given their new wives duties around the house. The first man had married a woman from Illinois and had told her that she was going to have to do the dishes and all the house cleaning. It took a couple of days, he said, but on the third day he came home to see a clean house and all the dishes washed and put away.

The second man had married a woman from Iowa. He had given his wife orders that she was to do all the cleaning, and the dishes, and the cooking. The first day he didn't see any results, but the next day he saw it was better. By the third day, he saw that the house was really clean, the dishes were done, and there was a huge dinner waiting for him on the table.

The third man had married a beautiful woman from New Jersey. He told her that her duties were to keep the house clean, wash the dishes, mow the lawn, do the laundry, and have hot meals on the table for him every day. **He said the first day he didn't see anything, the second day he didn't see anything, but by the third day some of the swelling had gone down and he could see a little out of his left eye**....enough to fix himself a sandwich and load the dishwasher.

Did you see that punchline coming? I doubt it. I think in view of the story, it was totally unexpected.

Strangely, there might be a connection here with the disciples of Jesus. Following Jesus' death on Good Friday, they might have wondered what they would do if He really came back to life. I mean Jesus had said it often enough so they should have remembered it. And in fact, the Gospels do say that they did remember it. But it seemed so far-fetched that they were in some sort of shock that it really could happen. I think that is why in so many of Jesus' appearances after the Resurrection, His own disciples and friends failed to recognize Him immediately. They were just too shocked to believe that it had actually happened, and like the joke's punchline, they weren't really expecting it.

So in today's Gospel we meet two of Jesus' disciples walking 7 miles from Jerusalem to the little village of Emmaus. **And Who comes and walks along with them but Jesus Himself!** And they don't recognize Him. In fact, they start telling Jesus about all the events that had happened. **(Jesus must have a great sense of humor....He even questions them about these events.)** And then Jesus starts explaining things to them from the Scriptures. And they are so enthralled that they invite Jesus to stay with them and share a meal with them. And so in the course of their discussion and the meal, they come to recognize Jesus as being alive and with them. They recognized Jesus in the breaking of the bread. As totally unexpected as it must have seemed to those two disciples on the road to Emmaus that day, it was actually true! Jesus really had risen from the dead and was walking along with them! He was there the whole time, and now they could see it!

Jesus died and rose from the dead so that you and I could share in His victory. Jesus WANTS us to share in His power and presence!

I hope you realize that Jesus has even given us a share in His own life because in His goodness He has allowed us to be baptized and become members of His holy Catholic Church. He is with us the whole time. He walks with us. He even guides us if we let Him.

I hope you realize that Jesus even gives us an exact location and place to come together to meet Him on a regular basis. That, after all, is what church is. It is a definite location and place where we can know for sure in Faith that Jesus is present and waiting to meet us. Have you ever just stopped by church for a few minutes? It's really easy to do, and Jesus in the Holy Eucharist is really here.

If in Faith, you know for certain that the Risen Lord Jesus with all His power and all His grace is here waiting for you, wouldn't you make the effort to be sure to be here and invite your family and friends to come too? Of course, you'd want to be here on Sundays with the whole community, but you'd probably want to get a little one-on-one time with the Lord too. You don't have to be a rocket scientist to realize what a wonderful gift Jesus is offering us.

And really all we have to do is to give the Lord a chance, place ourselves in His presence, and let Him do what He does best. He lets us share in His risen life. This week, think about the availability of the presence and the power of the Risen Christ....right here today and every day, and take advantage of it. And be grateful for it.

God bless you!

My Mom always thought I looked so holy on
My First Holy Communion Day back in 1955

Fourth Sunday of Easter - "A"

15 May 2011

FIRST READING: Acts 2:14, 36-41
PSALM: Psalm 23:1-6
SECOND READING: 1 Peter 2:20-25
GOSPEL: John 10:1-10

"The Lord is my Shepherd, there is nothing I shall want." (Psalm 23)

Another awesome week in and around Paradise! Back in April, FOX 5 NEWS taped a story about our little parish and our special relationship with the Riverside Casino here in Laughlin. There is something newsworthy and unique about being the only Catholic parish in Nevada, and maybe in the whole USA, or even the whole world that has its own commemorative casino chip and regularly celebrates Mass in a casino showroom. Fox reporter Matt DeLucia picked up on the story from an email I sent to Fox News and brought a photographer here on April 9th. They spent about 6 hours with me playing tourguide at the Riverside and during our 4:00 PM Mass. I am extremely grateful to the Riverside and to the Diocese of Las Vegas for allowing them to tape the segment and **it will air on Monday night during the 10:00 PM news**. The details are in our bulletin this week. You already know how much I love Laughlin, and I'm glad to share that love with even more people thanks to FOX 5 NEWS. If you get a chance to watch it, you'll probably see several people you know! And if you have the ability to record it for me, I'd love to get a copy or copies of it. Little by little, our secret Paradise is becoming known to the world!

I was up in Vegas for a couple of days this week with John Rotellini and a couple of friends from the University of Wyoming Class of 2011. John is a young magician/friend of mine. We did a mini-magic-marathon of shows to celebrate their graduation. I think we did 7 shows in 48 hours! I do know that I got to sleep one night at 3:30 AM, and I felt gratified that they were all just as tired as I was! John's girlfriend did not want to go up on stage during the shows. She even wrote to me before the trip asking me to try to prevent that from happening. I assured her that both John and I love to be up on stage, so if it ever came down to a choice between us missing out on going on stage in a magic show, or dragging her with us, she was definitely going on stage! I think she will eventually forgive us. **Bernie is another story**. He's 6'5" and looks like the guy on the brawny paper towel package. He definitely did not want to go up on stage, especially in a comedy magic routine where he had to wear a Marilyn Monroe-like mask and wave and blow a kiss at the audience. All I know is that John and I were sitting in the front row, and Bernie got picked to go on stage. He dutifully did what the comedian told him to do. He wore the mask, and on command would wave and blow a kiss at the audience.....and then he would just glare at John and me and shake his fist! It was fun.....for us.

Other than Father Peter across the river, I don't get to hang around with many priests, but Father Peter and I get out to eat lunch together almost every month. By the way, he's coming up on his 20th anniversary as pastor in Bullhead City next month. Now that's a record I would like to imitate!

Four pastors, taking a break one day, were sitting peacefully and talking. One of them said, **"You know, since all of us are such good friends, this might be a good time to discuss personal problems."** They all agreed that they would share some individual personal problem with the group. **"Well, I would like to share with you that I drink to excess,"** said one. There was a gasp from the other three. Then another spoke up, **"Since you were so honest, I'd like to say that my big problem is gambling. It's terrible, I know, but I can't quit."** Another gasp was heard. The third clergyman spoke up and said, **"I'm really troubled because I think I'm falling in love with someone else's wife."** More gasps were heard. But the fourth pastor remained silent. After a few minutes, the others coaxed him to open up and say something. **"The fact is,"** he said, **"I just don't know how to tell you about my problem."** "It's all right, brother," they said, **"Your secret is safe with us."** "Well, it's like this," he said, **"You see, I'm an incurable gossip."**

It's been said that every pastor ought to have six weeks of vacation each year, because if he's a really good shepherd, he deserves it, and if he is not a very good shepherd, his congregation deserves it.

I remember a few years ago, when I was leaving New Jersey, the Parish Pastoral Council hosted me a great farewell party for me, and some people seemed a little sad that I would be leaving. I tried to cheer them up with the knowledge that I was surely happy about going to the Diocese of Las Vegas and ultimately to Laughlin. But, I had a tearful woman come by my office. I asked why she was crying, and she told me that it was because I was leaving. I tried to cheer her up and even told her that the new pastor might be a better preacher than I am and that she might like the new pastor better than me. That made her cry even more. So I asked her why she was still crying, and she said **"That's what they told us the last time!"**

So why all the stories about pastors and my friends today? Today is traditionally called **GOOD SHEPHERD**

SUNDAY since the readings speak about Jesus as the Good Shepherd. In both the Old Testament and the New Testament, the Bible uses the image of a shepherd and his flock to describe the unique relationship of God to Israel, and of Christ to Christians. In the Catholic tradition, the pastor of a parish is viewed as a shepherd. But in reality, everyone who is entrusted with the care of others is sort of a shepherd too. So pastors, parents, teachers, doctors, nurses, scout leaders, real friends and so many others are all shepherds. We become GOOD shepherds by loving those entrusted to our care, by praying for them, by spending time with them, by working for their welfare, and by guarding them from physical and spiritual dangers.

Today's responsorial Psalm is the famous 23rd Psalm - **"The Lord is my Shepherd, there is nothing I shall want."**

It's a beautiful reminder of God's loving care for us throughout our lives. And in the Gospel today Jesus tells us **"I came so that they might have life and have it more abundantly."** This might be a good weekend to reflect a little on God's loving care and the abundant life God wants us to have. If we think about it, chances are that the way we learn to trust in God's loving care and share in God's abundant life is through our personal good shepherds - good family and good friends. They reach out to us, they listen to us, they touch our lives so powerfully. In fact, some psychologists state that we can get through anything in life if we only have a couple of good friends. The Bible speaks of friendship as a great treasure. He who finds a faithful friend has found an unfailing treasure.

A few questions to think about this week - Who are your friends? How have they shown you God's care and abundant life? How have you shown God's care and abundant life to them? How have you been a good shepherd to those in your care?

Remember your family and friends this weekend. Get in touch with at least one person who has been a good shepherd in your life, and thank him/her. It may seem like a small thing to do, but it's really important for us to recognize those who take care of us...and it's really important for us to try to take care of each other here along the banks of the beautiful Colorado River or back in our hometowns after our visit here.

God bless you!

Fifth Sunday of Easter - "A"

22 May 2011

FIRST READING: Acts 6:1-7
PSALM: Psalm 33:1-2, 4-5, 18-19
SECOND READING: 1 Peter 2:4-9
GOSPEL: John 14:1-12

Sorry, but I have no sermon for you today....I was sure the world was going to end today so I just didn't bother to write one!

Well, today (May 21st), the world was supposed to end through a series of giant earthquakes going around the world at 6:00 PM local time in each place. That means New York and New Jersey will be destroyed 3 hours before us, but it just didn't happen! One man took his life savings and spent $140,000 putting posters up in the New York City subway stations and bus stops reminding people that they were going to die today! Man, if I had $140,000 and knew that the world was going to end on Saturday, I certainly wouldn't be wasting it on posters! I am constantly amazed that members of an obscure minuscule sect could convince even some people about a disaster like they predicted. **There may be 52 of them somewhere in the world, but they surely aren't playing**

with a full deck! Why do people believe such things? It's like we're back in the jungles with Jim Jones again and the red Kool-Aid! Still can't figure out why people fall for such nonsense. However, just in case....I did eat an extra dessert last night. No sense dying on an empty stomach! :)

Had an interesting discussion with the homebuilders for my home here in Laughlin. I asked if they really had to include a range in the kitchen. They thought I was kidding and said that a gas range comes with the house. I said I could use another cabinet there more than a stove. So I asked if they could install an electric range instead. They said you just told us you didn't want a stove at all, so what good would an electric stove be? Well, I could pile stuff on top of it without worrying about it catching fire from the gas burners!

Actually, in view of the earthquake predictions for tonight, I was thinking of doing some cooking....SHAKE AND BAKE chicken might be appropriate!

The Fox 5 News broadcast about us on Monday night was really well done, and good publicity for Laughlin, for the Riverside and for the Catholic Church! In fact, at the diocesan priests' council meeting this week, we were mentioned by another priest as being responsible for some really good upbeat and positive news coverage for the Catholic Church in the Diocese of Las Vegas! I'm enjoying my 15 minutes of fame. Some of my more sarcastic friends have called and left messages for **"Father Hollywood"** this week! I hope Laughlin picks up a few extra visitors because of the broadcast. We surely want to share Paradise!

On Wednesday, I will celebrate my 37th anniversary as a priest and that will be **Mass #18480** for me! I'll be up in Vegas for that day, but I promise I'll be thinking of you. Being assigned here with you in Paradise is really my dream come true, and I thank God for this assignment every day! You and my family have made me the happiest priest in the entire world!

Two thoughts always come to my mind whenever I read today's Gospel from St. John. One is a thought that some of you may share - this Gospel reminds me of funerals because it is so frequently chosen as the reading at many Catholic funerals. It's a beautiful and comforting reminder of the Lord's care for us when we pass from this life into eternity.

The other thought is a more personal one that comes back to me from my past. When I was about to be ordained as a priest in 1974, I had made arrangements for my First Mass to be at my home parish of Our Lady of Mercy in Park Ridge and a dinner for several hundred people to be at the brand new Ramada Inn in Montvale. Now a First Mass dinner is kind of like a wedding reception, except that there is no bride to do the details! You should have seen me doing the seating plan! **I always felt that you can seat people in one of two ways: so that they have fun OR so that you have fun watching them! You can guess which one I chose!**

Well, I got kind of stressed and I recall really being picky over details with the new banquet manager at the Ramada - Herb Meushaw. But Herb was really patient with me each time I called with some minor detail. Except for one time....the night before I was ordained, I had a final thought on the meal, so I called Herb. He let me talk for a few seconds and then said, **"Charlie, what's going to happen to you tomorrow morning?"** I thought he was trying to distract me, but he repeated it, **"Charlie, what's going to happen to you tomorrow morning?"** I said, **"I'm going to be ordained a priest." "Do you think you'll be sent to a parish?"** I said **"Yes." "Do you think you'll ever preach to your people on a Sunday?"** I said" **"Yes." "Do you think you'll ever tell them to have faith?"** I said **"Yes."**

"Well, then have a little faith in me!" and with that he hung up the phone. When I arrived for the dinner, he told me to just go in and relax. He said he had had a nightmare the night before, thinking I had showed up early and he caught me in the kitchen straightening the cherry stems on the fruit cocktails!

I've never forgotten Herb's reminder: **"HAVE A LITTLE FAITH IN ME!"** and I think there is a good lesson in that for all of us.

Jesus said to His disciples: **"Do not let your hearts be troubled. You have faith in God; have faith also in Me."** That's good and sound advice for us not only at the time of death, but perhaps even more during the time of life here on earth.

When things happen in our lives, things that may not even be our own fault, are we secure enough to still have faith in Jesus? Do we still believe that Jesus is in control of the world and that we are still secure in His embrace?

There is nothing at all that is going on that is outside of the scope of God's care. Whether we think of wars and terrorism at home or in foreign countries, or whether we think of problems and changes in the church, or whether we think of problems within our own communities or within our own families with disease or loss of employment or disappointment with the ways things may have turned out in some other areas of life. **NOTHING is beyond God's care.**

Faith isn't going through life without problems. Faith is knowing that God stands with us even in our problems. Do we turn to God first, or do we sometimes come to Him only when we have tried everything else? Admit it, we've all done that sometime in our lives!

Herb's comment to me dates back less than 37 years, but down through the centuries God has been saying pretty much the same thing: **"HAVE A LITTLE FAITH IN ME!"** This week maybe we can ask God in prayer for the gift of a stronger faith in Him. Maybe we can turn over some of the nagging and specific problems in our lives to God and trust that He will always do His part. It's not easy to let go of our problems and issues, but God asks us to trust that He knows how to handle them better than we do.

As I once wrote in our bulletin: **"Before you go to sleep at night, give your problems to God. He's going to be up all night anyway!"**

God bless you!

Sixth Sunday of Easter - "A"

29 May 2011

FIRST READING: Acts 8:5-8, 14-17
PSALM: Psalm 66:1-7, 16, 20
SECOND READING: 1 Peter 3:15-18
GOSPEL: John 14:15-21

"What does Memorial Day mean to you?"

Another really awesome week here in Paradise! One of the parishioners gave me a whole fresh-baked loaf of bread. It smelled so wonderful! And it tasted even better! I may not be able to cook, but I sure do enjoy home-cooked items like that! I feel it's my duty to not only eat them, but to totally enjoy them to show my gratitude to the giver. I do my best!

My friend Rob joined a Boot Camp gym program. He gets up at 5AM to be at the gym before 6AM, and then does crazy workouts for an hour. I'm impressed and amazed, but have no intention of joining him! We both agree that we need to take care of our bodies because they are temples of the Lord. It just that his is more like a church, while I think of mine more as a large basilica!

Had dinner with comedy magician Mike Hammer on Wednesday night after his show. He does a routine which involves putting an old white suit coat on an audience volunteer and commenting that it makes her look like a Las Vegas performer from 1932. And he usually follows that with **"Just like you remember, Charlie, right?"** We kid with each other so much during his show that the audience never quite believes I'm a priest and sometimes thinks I'm part of the show. We laugh and talk so much during dinner that it's hard to actually finish our meals! We were joined by a couple of other friends and magicians this week and they commented that we should get our own show and go on tour as a comedy magic act! I think I'll keep my job here in Laughlin! But it's fun to think about having options! By the way, Mike really likes my book. He says he always keeps it handy. Not to read, but he uses it as a coaster and a table-brace!

Speaking of options, one of Mike's other jobs is as a ring-announcer for the UFC competitions here in Vegas. Kind of strange, but I like stuff like that. When I was a kid, I loved professional wrestling and my favorite wrestler was **THE ULTIMATE WARRIOR**. He was huge! And he had warpaint on his face and body. Years later, I learned that he was only a pro-wrestler as a sideline. He was really a dentist. From then on, every time I went to my dentist, I would imagine what it would be like to have the Ultimate Warrior working on my teeth.

Speaking of options, I think Memorial Day presents us with some serious options. I was on the internet this week and found a site promoting a NATIONAL MEMENT OF

REMEMRBRANCE at 3:00 PM on Memorial Day. Funny, but I don't recall seeing this in the newspapers, or hearing about it from the diocese, or even noticing it on TV or radio. But it really is an awesome idea - that at 3:00 P.M. on Memorial Day, we should all stop for just a moment and in our own way remember the sacrifice of those who have died serving our country.

Has Memorial Day become just an extra holiday from work or school? Have we made it more a time to hit the shopping malls or go to river? Once this was not so. Back a few decades, our nation honored those who had died in its service on the 30th of May, and not on a day conveniently tacked onto the nearest two-day weekend to create a three-day holiday. And on May 30th, which was then called **DECORATION DAY**, Americans marched in or watched parades in virtually every little town and big city, and then went on to the cemeteries to place flags on the graves of those who had died defending our nation.

Supposedly, a little girl was asked **"What does Memorial Day mean to you?"** And she replied, **"That's the day the pool opens."** Perhaps it really is time to put the

"**Memorial**" back into Memorial Day. So on Monday at 3PM or whenever you can, just pause for a moment wherever you are, and remember the sacrifices of the men and women throughout our American history who have given their lives so that you and I could live in freedom, so that we could go to our pools, or to the river, or to the malls. Their dedication to duty and honor and integrity is worth remembering and worth honoring. **Our liberty comes at a price, a great price.** With honor and pride, we prayerfully remember those who died in the Revolutionary War, the War of 1812, the Mexican War, the Civil War, the Spanish American War, World War I, World War II, the Korean War, The Vietnam War, The Persian Gulf War, Desert Storm and all the various conflicts, incidents and peacekeeping missions including the current War on Terrorism. And may we also remember all those veterans who have served and survived. And those who are POW's or MIA's still And may we be mindful of those who currently serve in our **ARMY, NAVY, AIR FORCE, MARINES and COAST GUARD** today, especially those whose lives are at risk in Afghanistan and Iraq, and places all over the globe. We remember and pray for all those who serve our nation.

For us as Catholics, the whole idea of a memorial remembrance is so close to our hearts and so much a part of our Faith. We remember the words of God to us in the Bible, we remember God's actions in our lives in the seven sacraments. Every Mass is for us a memorial, a remembrance of what God has done for us. Jesus even tells us at the consecration of every Mass - **"Do this in memory of Me"** - and Jesus really meant what He said. He told us that the bread and wine we offer at Mass are changed into the **BODY AND BLOOD OF JESUS CHRIST** through the words of the priest. This is one of our most significant and unique beliefs as Roman Catholics. So just as every Sunday is a special memorial for us as Catholics, this Monday is a special memorial for us as Americans.

It's time to put the "MEMORIAL" back into MEMORIAL DAY.

God bless you!

322

Ascension of the Lord

5 June 2011

FIRST READING: Acts 1:1-11
PSALM: Psalm 47:2-3, 6-9
SECOND READING: Ephesians 1:17-23
GOSPEL: Matthew 28:16-20

Have you ever heard of something called the GREAT COMMISSION?

What a great week here in Paradise! Within the past 7 days, the builders have framed the walls of my new house, put in the windows and started tiling the roof! I think it is the only house currently being constructed in Laughlin so it is getting a lot of attention. The saleslady at the model said she has people stopping in all the time wanting to "see what Father Charlie's house will look like." And so many of our parishioners are taking pictures of the construction that I'm wondering if the workmen might be getting a little nervous. Maybe they will be extra-careful what they do since they know someone will have photographic proof of everything!

Meanwhile, back at the rectory, I had a little excitement. On Thursday afternoon, I found a snake in my garage. If anyone ever tells you, **"Don't worry, it's more scared** than you are," don't believe them! I made it from the door into my car without my feet even touching the ground! And when I backed out, I couldn't see the snake anymore, so I guess it is either somewhere in my garage or somewhere outside the house. People asked me what it looked like....believe me, I was moving too fast to notice much about it other than it was a snake! I figure it is somewhere between a deadly diamondback rattler or a harmless gopher snake. **I'm kind of hoping that I never see it again!** But, you know, I shouldn't be surprised. After all, this is Paradise, and the original Paradise had a snake too!

But Eve must have been braver than I am to stop and talk to it!

While I'm not fond of snakes, people who know me know that I like **OWLS**. I've liked them since I was a kid. I've always been sort of a "night-owl" myself! At one point, I had over 2000 things with owls on them! I was at a meeting once in San Antonio, Texas, and a group of my friends who are Baptist ministers took me out for dinner one night.

They said they had found the perfect place for us to eat and that I would love it! Well, we walked past a few country music bars (I love country music), but we didn't go into any of them. And we walked past some Italian restaurants, but we didn't go into them. Finally, we went into this one place and I was really surprised. Remember, the group I was with were all Baptist ministers, who didn't drink alcohol. And the place they brought me to that night was **HOOTERS**. The one and only time I have eaten in a **HOOTERS** was with a group of Baptist ministers who don't drink! They told me they were so happy because they had found an entire restaurant devoted to **OWLS**! Boy, were they surprised!

Have you ever heard of something called the **GREAT COMMISSION**? It's a very popular expression in theology, and is contained in today's Gospel.

A really good friend of mine, who happens to be one of the Baptist ministers who took me to **HOOTERS**, once preached an hour-long sermon on the **GREAT COMMISSION**. He told me that his Baptist congregation in Louisiana would feel cheated if he didn't preach for at least an hour! I told him that a Catholic congregation would have a different view of a sermon that long! I promise I won't preach an hour-long sermon to you today. But I do want to remind you of what the **GREAT COMMISSION** is.

It is Jesus' final instructions to His Apostles and disciples, just before He ascended into heaven. St. Matthew in today's gospel spells it out clearly. Jesus said to them: "**All power in heaven and on earth has been given to Me. Go, therefore, and make disciples of all nations, baptizing them in the name of the Father and of the Son and of the Holy Spirit, teaching them to observe all that I have commanded you. And, behold, I am with you always, until the end of the age.**" The **GREAT COMMISSION** is to take what we have learned from Jesus and to share it with the world around us.

Today as we celebrate Jesus' Ascension into heaven, think about the **GREAT COMMISSION**. You and I are the ones who are Jesus' disciples in the world today. We're the ones who are supposed to spread His message with our lives and our words. We're the ones who are carrying on the work the Jesus began so many centuries ago. We're the ones who are now supposed to be fulfilling the **GREAT COMMISSION**. We believe in Jesus' teachings because those who came before us did their part. Now it's our turn.

I did that in a lot less than an hour-long sermon! I hope you don't feel cheated because it only took a few minutes! **This is not new material**. This is just a reminder of what all of us should be doing already. We are Jesus' disciples in the world today. It is up to us to continue His work. It's as simple as that! This week, resolve to tell someone or show someone what your Faith prompts you to do. Because a Faith that is worth having is a Faith that is worth living, and sharing!

God bless you!

Pentecost

12 June 2011

FIRST READING: Acts 2:1-11
PSALM: Psalm 104:1, 24, 29-31, 34
SECOND READING: 1 Corinthians 12:3-7, 12-13
GOSPEL: John 20:19-23

"Who is the least likely person for you to be sitting next to on an airplane and having this conversation?"

It's been another amazing week here in Paradise! I was away for part of the week on retreat near San Francisco with most of the priests of the Diocese of Las Vegas. **I froze the whole time!** Give me 100+ degrees anytime over damp cold weather! I was sleeping in sweat pants and socks just to keep warm! And I washed out a shirt in the sink....and two days later it was still damp! **They gave me the room right next to the bishop.** Not sure if he was supposed to keep an eye on me or not! The retreat was really good! Our speaker was Bishop Nicholas Samra, an Eastern Rite bishop originally from New Jersey (so two of us have made it out!). A lot of what he said focused on the idea that Eastern thought is much more spiritual than Western thought which tends to be much more legal. It was refreshing, and perfect for the retreat. Father John

Assalone and I not only stayed awake for the talks, but we actually only texted each other ONCE during the retreat! We must be getting more obedient, and reverent, and holy!

On my flight home from San Francisco to Las Vegas, the Southwest Airlines flight was completely full. I got one of the coveted aisle seats, and a pretty young female got the window seat in our row. As the plane was filling up, a young guy came down the aisle, saw the girl, and dove for the middle seat. Well, the girl wasn't interested in him, she turned towards the window and fell asleep! So he was now stuck in the middle seat, with no one to talk to but me! Poor guy! He had just moved to San Francisco from Chicago and was working as a restaurant manager. After we talked for awhile, he told me that I seemed like a **"personable guy"** so he asked what I did for a living after I escaped from New Jersey. I said he'd never guess. Well, he told me he liked playing 20 questions, and he was really good at it. In fact, he said he would probably figure out my career in less than 10 questions. I said, **"Give it a try!"** I even sweetened the pot and told him that if he got it in 20 questions, I would treat him to dinner and a magic show the next time he came to Vegas.

Well, after the first ten questions, he was really struggling. He ruled out that I was a doctor, a lawyer, a scientist, a CEO, an FBI agent, a Microsoft product developer (I can barely work my cellphone!). He asked me if my job involved **"extreme danger"**, and I replied **"Not for me!"** He asked if I were an entertainer. I said I thought I was, but that really isn't in my job description. At question 19, he asked if I were a prison warden. I offered to give him a hint for question 20....I said **"Who is the least likely person for you to be sitting next to on an airplane having this conversation with?"** That usually gives it away....sad, but true, since way too many people think that priests are no fun! He looked at me and said: **"An Air Traffic Controller!"** I asked why that would be the least likely person for him to be having this conversation with on an airplane, and he said because if you were an Air Traffic Controller, you should be on the ground!

He was surprised to find out I was a priest, and it turns out that he was a Catholic, just hadn't talked to a priest since he was 13! We're doing dinner and a magic show in a few months when he comes back to Vegas. Even though he didn't guess my job correctly, he was still a fun person to make the flight go by quickly.

This weekend, we celebrate Pentecost, the sending of the Holy Spirit on the Church – 50 days after Easter. If we were to ask 20 questions about the Holy Spirit, we would still not understand fully what His Presence means. Is the Holy Spirit God? YES. Does He live within each one of us?

YES. Do we have a clue as to HOW He does that? NO. Is it important that He lives within us? YES. And the list could go on and on.

On retreat this week, I thought about how much help we receive from God each and every day of our lives. We can be strong because we know God is with us and wants only the best for us. He stands behind us to strengthen us, He goes ahead of us to lead us. He stands beside us to give us Someone to lean on. And He lives within us to fill us with His Spirit so we can learn to think and act like God.

No matter what is going on in our lives right now, no matter how amazing or horrifying it might be, we can count on God's Holy Spirit to always be with us. We don't really have to understand exactly HOW, we just need to appreciate that somehow it happens.

When you do something that you know you couldn't do just on your own, that's the Holy Spirit.

When you feel an urge to go out of your way to offer help to someone, that's the Holy Spirit.

When you find the strength to avoid some sin or temptation, that's the Holy Spirit.

Even when you pray and sometimes struggle to find the right words, that's the Holy Spirit.

With Pentecost, the Easter Season comes to an end, but God's Holy Spirit remains with us always. Happy Pentecost!

God bless you!

Most Holy Trinity

19 June 2011

FIRST READING: Exodus 34:4-6, 8-9
PSALM: Daniel 3:52-55
SECOND READING: 2 Corinthians 13:11-13
GOSPEL: John 3:16-18

I immediately asked if I could bring my penguin.

Best wishes for Father's Day to all our fathers, Godfathers, grandfathers, step-fathers, adopted fathers, and all those other men who have been father-like to us in the course of our lives.

I thought about my own father a lot recently, but not because of Father's Day. You see, I was invited to be the Co - Master of Ceremonies at the Annual Community Achievement Awards last weekend, and it's the only black-tie affair in Laughlin each year. Of course, I was honored to be asked, and I immediately asked if I could bring my penguin. They thought I was kidding, but I insisted that my penguin was already dressed in black and white and should come to the affair with me. Back in 1957, my father was a Marine Surveyor for the government and worked out of Fort Hamilton in Brooklyn, NY. One of the ships was part of International

Geophysical Year 1957, and my father arranged for me to receive one of the two penguins they brought back. Unfortunately, the penguins died on the ship, so they were taxidermied and I got one of them. I think my Mom was glad the penguin was dead....she had enough problems with my pet alligator so a penguin would have been a bit too much trouble! At any rate, I was always a winner at show-and-tell in school, since it was really hard to beat out a real stuffed penguin! And last weekend, I had to carry my penguin through the casino on my way to and from the awards dinner. You should have seen the look on people's faces seeing a priest carrying a penguin! Some people asked me if it were my lucky charm (and I told them I placed it on top of the slot machine I was playing). Tons of very pretty females came over and wanted to pet my penguin (I think I may rent it out for young single guys to use when they want to meet women!). And I think I stopped a few people from drinking that night (after all, once you've seen a priest with a penguin in a casino, you've got to think you've had one too many drinks!) **So, thanks, Dad, for all the fun last weekend!**

Some people have told me that I rarely speak about my father. My father died of cancer when he was only 55 and when I was just in my teens, so he wasn't around for any of my adult life. I do remember a few scenes from our past, besides the penguin, some of which I'll mention.

I can vividly remember going into work with him on some days and walking around the huge engine rooms of the government ships. And going out for pizza with him when I was a little kid on Saturday nights. We used to buy the Sunday papers at Midnight, and then sit on the living room floor eating and reading them. And we always made it up for Mass on Sunday morning!

I don't know if teens will still relate to this scenario, but when I got my driver's license at age 17, I quickly discovered that I could drive with my mother in the car, but not with my father. My Mom would just sit quietly, cringe, and grasp for the door handle or dashboard and close her eyes. My father would yell instructions. "Don't do that....Move into that lane now....slow down.....speed up." I once pulled off the Long Island Expressway with him, got out of the car and said, "You drive. I'm never driving with you in the car again!"

When he got sick in the 1960's, I remember taking care of him at home and trying to give my mother a break now and then so she could go out. My advice to kids....if you still have your fathers around. Today would be a great day to tell them you're glad they're part of your lives.

Today is also TRINITY SUNDAY, a yearly commemoration of the Holy Trinity – Father, Son and Holy Spirit. Years ago, when I was a teacher at a Catholic

School, I explained to my 7th grade class that this was a
great mystery in our Catholic Faith which no one really
understands. I told them about some of the great saints
who had tried to describe it. Like St. Patrick, who used
the three leaves on the Irish shamrock to show how
three leaves could be one shamrock. Or St. John Vianney
who used the candles in his church to explain that a flame
has color, shape and heat, but is still only one flame. Or
he would hold up a glass of water, and explain how the
contents could be water, or steam or ice, and yet still be
water. I told my students that they would never
understand it, but I made their homework assignment
that night to be writing out their explanation of the Holy
Trinity. They came up with all sorts of cool examples,
determined to prove me wrong and show me that they
could understand the Holy Trinity! One kid said it was like
an egg – shell, yolk and white, yet still only one egg.
Another brought in a three-leafed plant to imitate St.
Patrick's example. The only problem was that New Jersey
didn't have shamrocks, it was poison ivy that he brought
in!

God reaches us in a variety of ways! Today's feast is
called **TRINITY SUNDAY**, a day on which we celebrate
the MYSTERY OF THE HOLY TRINITY - THE MYSTERY
OF THREE PERSONS IN ONE GOD. It's a mystery
because we don't fully understand it, but we do
experience it, and every Sunday we say in the CREED

that we believe in the FATHER, and the SON, and the HOLY SPIRIT. We experience God in our lives in many ways that reflect the TRINITY.

God is a loving and caring parent, a Father in the truest and most beautiful sense of the word. He created the world and He holds it in existence. He is all-powerful.

God is Jesus, a true human being, a person like us in all things but sin, a warm and personal friend to each one of us. He is close to us.

God is the Holy Spirit, an all-pervading presence, a power who enlightens our minds and strengthens our wills to do good and to avoid evil. He is God's gift of wisdom to each one of us.

Each one of us has his/her own way of relating to God or thinking about God. The TRINITY reminds us that we all need to relate to God in His WHOLENESS. He is a loving and caring Father, but He is also an AWESOME JUDGE who controls the entire universe. In Jesus, He is a truly human person like us, but He is **never** "just like us." He is always God among us. As the Holy Spirit, He is God's wisdom in the world, but He works through us and through others to share His wisdom and guidance. We need to pay attention to Him.

God is greater and larger than any of our categories for Him. He is beyond our categories of TIME and SPACE. He is the God who created the world, Who freed His people from slavery at the time of Moses, Who has in our own time chosen us as His own sons and daughters, and Who shares His own Spirit with us. He will remain with us always.

The simple sign of the cross which we make so often (and sometimes so very carelessly) is a powerful reminder that God always remains a mystery to us. He is Someone greater than we can ever imagine, Someone who cannot be confined to our narrow categories and our very limited minds. God has made each one of us in His own image. We should never reverse things and try to make our God just like us. **God is higher, deeper, wider than even the universe itself**....and for some reason in His eternal plan, God wants to be close to us. Think of that the next time you make the sign of the cross. God wants to be close to you.

In the Name of the Father, and of the Son, and of the Holy Spirit.

Amen!

God bless you!

Corpus Christi – "A"

26 June 2011

FIRST READING: Deuteronomy 8:2-3, 14-16
PSALM: Psalm 147:12-15, 19-20
SECOND READING: 1 Corinthians 10:16-17
GOSPEL: John 6:51-58

Looking for how to make it across this raging river we call life?

Another amazing week here in Paradise! Father John texted me and said that when he got home to St. Francis from the retreat, he got asked if he and I had behaved on retreat, or did we get into trouble for our texting during the sessions. I said I got the same type of questions here, so I guess we have a reputation to uphold! And after showing my stuffed penguin at the Masses last weekend, I got criticized by some of our parishioners. No for having a penguin at Mass, but for not charging $5 a picture when people wanted to have a photo with the penguin! Guess I missed that opportunity!

Went for a haircut this week here in Laughlin, and that's always a wonderful experience! There's something about getting my hair shampooed on these somewhat warm days! As the stylist gently rubs the shampoo into my hair, I just glaze over and almost fall asleep, it is so relaxing! After the haircut, she said she wanted to give me something because I'm so nice. So she gave me a bottle of shampoo to take home. **What a great gift! When I got home, I read the label and it is called "GROW SHAMPOO"..."DESIGNED TO STOP MEN'S HAIR LOSS".**

Heard about a new taste treat that is becoming really popular at fairs and events: Deep-fried Kool-Aid. It's Kool-Aid powder mixed with some flour and water and deep-fried! Sells for $5.95 for 5 little balls of it. Got to try that someday!

And I received a wonderful gift for my new house from Deacon Dan and Pixie. Normally, I like to pick out decorations for myself, but this one is perfect and will have a place of honor in my new house. It's a plaque that reads: **"I only have a kitchen because it came with the house!"** Golly, they know me too well!

And on Friday night, I went over to Harrah's for a new comedy club. A buddy of mine – Zach Risen – is the MC for it and I wanted to see his act. Zach is probably the skinniest guy I know and it was fun to hear him joking about his **"weight problem"** and how hard it is for him to get a date! He claims that people hate him for trying to put on weight, and that for some reason girls want to be with a guy who actually weighs more than they do! He gets no sympathy from me!

The other comic on the bill this week is a guy named Butch Bradley. I had never heard of him, but I liked the fact that he goes over to entertain our troops. In fact, on his website he writes: "I am not pro-war, but I am pro-soldier!" What a great outlook! He told how strange it was to be driving to Laughlin....down that dirt road and past all the crosses. His girlfriend asked him about it, and he said "those are the people who didn't make it". There were more of us when we left Vegas, but we survived and made it to Laughlin! The funny thing is that he kept joking about Laughlin – where dreams come true! Of course, I had to email him and tell him that I wrote a book with that title and he needs to learn some more about our Paradise!

He did have several really funny routines about how women never get lost, but men do! He said you never hear a news report about search parties looking for groups of women who got lost, but they're always looking for groups of guys who head out to snowmobile in an avalanche zone, or who get lost in a forest. It reminded me of a story I once heard:

The story is told of three men who faced a violently raging river and had to get across it. The first man prayed to God, "Dear God, give me the strength to get across this raging river." And he dived into the water and 10 hours later had made it across the water by swimming with all his might. The second man prayed to God. "Dear God, give me the strength and the tools to get across this raging river." And suddenly a rowboat appeared and he rowed across the raging river in about 2 hours. The third man prayed to God, "Dear God, give me the strength and the tools and the intelligence to get across this raging river." And suddenly, God changed him into a woman, and he took out the map, saw that there was a bridge about 15 yards up stream and calmly walked across in about 10 minutes.

It's kind of an insane tradition that men do not want to look at maps or ask for directions no matter what the situation. And that's really too bad because sometimes there really are important pieces of information given in the directions that we need to know, and that can save us a lot of useless effort.

The Bible is a set of directions given to us by God to guide us on our journey through life. In fact, someone once commented that even the word **BIBLE** can be seen as an acronym for **BASIC INSTRUCTIONS BEFORE LEAVING EARTH**. It tells us a lot about God and a lot about life.

Today's feast of CORPUS CHRISTI, the BODY AND BLOOD OF CHRIST, calls to mind a very important Biblical and Catholic truth - that Jesus really meant what He said. He told us that the bread and wine we offer at Mass are changed into the BODY AND BLOOD OF JESUS CHRIST through the words of the priest. This is one of our most significant and unique beliefs as Roman Catholics. We really do believe in the REAL PRESENCE of JESUS CHRIST in the Holy Eucharist.

Several things (directions) come to mind because of this wonderful Catholic belief. We really believe that Jesus remains in our church buildings in our tabernacles 24 hours a day, 7 days a week. We really believe that as Roman Catholics in the state of grace that we are allowed (encouraged) to receive God Himself in Holy Communion. And we believe that none of this would be possible without the existence of an ordained priesthood. And we really believe that Jesus Christ meant what He said when He told us that He would not abandon us, but would remain with us until the end of time. As Jesus says in today's Gospel: **"Amen, amen, I say to you, unless you eat the flesh of the Son of Man and drink His blood, you do not have life within you....Whoever eats My flesh and drinks My blood remains in Me and I in him....Whoever eats this bread will live forever."**

346

Looking for how to make it across this raging river we call life? Trying to figure out how to best use our strength and tools and intelligence in this life? Just follow the directions in the Bible. Come to Jesus in the Holy Eucharist. Besides Mass on Sunday which is an obligation, wouldn't it be wonderful if we could spend some time with Jesus in the Blessed Sacrament during the week? Surely we have plenty of people and situations to pray for so we should have lots of things to talk over with the Lord. He's here, waiting for us to get to know Him better. All we have to do is follow His directions.

God bless you!

14th Sunday in Ordinary Time - "A"

3 July 2011

FIRST READING: Zechariah 9:9-10
PSALM: Psalm 145:1-2, 8-11, 13-14
SECOND READING: Romans 8:9, 11-13
GOSPEL: Matthew 11:25-30

"We hold these truths to be self-evident….."
(Declaration of Independence)

What an amazing week we had here in Paradise. Our trip to see the play "**GREASE**" in Utah was a great success! 35 people enjoyed the sights and sounds of an awesome outdoor production of "**GREASE**". And last weekend, I mentioned that my friend Zach was the MC at the Comedy Club at Harrah's here in Laughlin on summer weekends. I talked a little about him, and apparently a number of people went over to see the show. I know this because on Sunday night, I got an email from Zach telling me that it was the strangest thing, but lots of people were coming up to him after the show and asking him if he really knew me! Why is it so hard to believe that I could really know some cool people? I went back to the comedy club on Friday night and I learned a great idea from this week's guest comic. He was talking about how his girlfriend was not impressed when she came over to dinner to see that he had prepared it in a microwave. He said he had figured out a great plan. He put his microwave into his oven, and now when she comes over and asks about dinner, he just opens the oven door and remarks, **"It's almost ready!"** Now that's a great idea!

It's a hot, soon to be very hot, 4th of July weekend. I don't need to give a long sermon today, and you don't need to sit for one. But I thought I'd point out a little inspiration for this weekend as we celebrate our 235th birthday as a free and independent nation. And I found this inspiration in **three** sources: The Declaration of Independence, an email from a friend, and today's Gospel.

The Declaration of Independence, which was signed 235 years ago, begins with these words: **"We hold these truths to be self-evident, that all men are created equal, that they are endowed by their Creator with certain unalienable Rights, that among these are Life, Liberty, and the pursuit of Happiness."** 235 years later, we all need to remember that from the very beginning, our nation has acknowledged that there is a **CREATOR**, and that He is the Source of our rights. And that we are all endowed by our Creator with the right to **LIFE, LIBERTY** and the **PURSUIT OF HAPPINESS**. The Declaration of Independence states that all of this is **SELF-EVIDENT**, meaning any thinking person should be able to see it.

So as we celebrate this 4th of July weekend, it's good for us to give thanks to our **CREATOR**, and to thank Him for giving us **LIFE**, and **LIBERTY**, and allowing us to pursue **HAPPINESS**. It should be **SELF-EVIDENT** to all of us that God has given us so very much in the course of our lives.

My friend, Rick, sent me an email with a very profound bit of wisdom in it to share.

Too many people put off something that brings them happiness just because they haven't thought about it, don't have it on their schedule, didn't know it was coming, or are too rigid to depart from their routine.

I got to thinking one day about all those people on the Titanic who passed up dessert at dinner that fateful night. From then on, I've tried to be more flexible.

How many women will eat at home because their husband didn't suggest going out to dinner until **AFTER** something had already been thawed? Does the word **"REFRIGERATION"** mean nothing to you?

How often have your kids dropped in to talk and sat in silence while you watched "JEOPARDY" on TV?

Because we Americans cram so much into our lives, we tend to schedule everything. We wait for conditions to be perfect before we act.

We'll go and visit the grandparents when we get Steve toilet-trained. We'll entertain when we replace the living-room carpet. We'll go on that vacation when we get two more kids through college.

Life has a way of accelerating as we get older. The days get shorter and the list of promises gets longer. And one morning we wake up and all we have to show for our lives is a litany of **"I'm going to"** or **"I plan on"** or **"Someday, when things settle down a bit."**

My lips have not touched ice cream in 10 years. I love ice cream. It's just that I might as well apply it directly to my stomach with a spatula and eliminate the digestive process. The other day I stopped the car and bought a triple-scoop. If my car had hit an iceberg on the way home, I would have died happy.

Now go and have a nice day. Do something you **WANT** to, not something you **HAVE** to. If you were going to die soon and had only one phone call you could make, who would you call and what would you say? And why are you waiting to do it?

In today's Gospel from St. Matthew, the confidence of Jesus is **SELF-EVIDENT**. He knows the Father, and He knows that He came to us to reveal to us our relationship with God our Father. He promises that God our Father will always accept us and refresh us: **"Come to me, all you who labor and are burdened, and I will give you rest."**

Many centuries later as we look back at the Faith of Jesus disciples, it should be **SELF-EVIDENT** to us that they came to know that there was no other place to go, no other person to turn to Who could lead them. So they followed Jesus.

And that's what should be so inspirational to us today. We live in a country where we can freely come to God in worship. And like the disciples in today's Gospel, we know He has something to offer us that no one else has. He can help us in ways that no one else can. It's good to think about this too.

May God bless each one of us with the **SELF-EVIDENT FAITH** we see in today's Gospel, with the foresight and conviction of our American Founding Fathers, and with the determination to make each day of our lives an opportunity for pursuing the happiness and fulfillment that God wants us to have. God bless you, and have a Happy 4th of July this week!

God bless you!

Vincent April and Charlie – old friends!

Charlie and Ses Carny at River Run!

Is it a priest, or is it a shaman?

Dinner with Pat

Memories of THE PUNISHER!

Made in the USA
Middletown, DE
22 April 2024

53349464R00199